About the Author

Tara Lynne Groth is a freelance writer in have appeared in magazines and newspap She has written for trade and consumer pu *Produce Business, Blue Ridge Country, Durham* referenced in this book. She resigned from been running her writing business ever sinc of journalism, she founded and organizes Triangle Writers and Asheville Writers, and co-organizes Living Poetry, the largest group of poets in the Raleigh area. She is a proponent of writers being compensated for their work, and pays guest contributors on her blog Write Naked (www.writenaked.net). Write Naked breaks down the misconceptions people have about freelance life and features posts on publishing and book marketing, plus interviews with literary agents, publishers, poets and more. She tweets at @writenaked.

www.taralynnegroth.com

Want updates about freelancing? Scan the code to sign up for Tara Lynne's monthly newsletter.

Magazine Queries That Worked: Build Income and Authority With Freelance Journalism

By Tara Lynne Groth

Magazine Queries That Worked: Build Income and Authority With Freelance Journalism, © 2017 Tara Lynne Groth.

ISBN 978-0-692-91177-8

Contents

My Background: Early Days of Journalism

Getting paid to write had been a mystery to me until a random visit to the library in downtown Cary, North Carolina, in 2009. Until that point, any journalistic writing I had done had been unpaid. Plus, four years had passed since I'd written a feature-length article.

My only experiences with journalism until then included more than 40 articles in a liberal campus newspaper, *The Stony Brook Press*, when I was a student at Stony Brook University on Long Island, New York, where I majored in cinema and cultural studies. I had also published an editorial in the *Providence Journal*, a major newspaper in Rhode Island with a circulation of about 70,000. The latter was published when I was just 17, not quite the age for my legal adult life, but I was a college freshman at the time.

With regard to journalism, I was intrigued initially with the storytelling. I loved learning others' motivations, discovering unique story angles and gathering all these details into a concise narrative for others to read and connect with. I had the opportunity to write for the *Stony Brook Press*—as they're open to submissions from any student, as far as I recall—so I penned movie reviews and social commentary. Although it got me into the write-complete-submit groove, none of my submissions ever got sent back for edits. The same with that editorial I published freshman year—it too was published verbatim. Years later, when I wrote my first paid feature, a cover story for a local publication in North Carolina, I didn't know what to expect. Fortunately, they requested no revisions either… but that was not the case for other markets, as I later discovered!

After I graduated college, like so many other people with degrees in the arts, I got a job in a field completely unrelated to my passion and studies. I was the public relations director for a real estate office just a few miles from my alma mater. I had worked at the office part-time throughout college, and they made me a full-time offer upon my graduation. I embraced the job. Each of the homes had a story to tell, and the homeowners and buyers had their own interesting narratives. Although I wrote property descriptions and shot virtual tours, they were anemic versions of writing and filmmaking. My degree and long-time interests felt wasted.

Meanwhile, I wrote for and managed advertising for a short-lived newspaper called *The Suffolk Standard* that a few members of the *Press* had formed. It reached a circulation of about 20,000 across parts of Long Island. After the paper folded, I didn't have another outlet for journalism. The term "freelance journalist" was not part of my vocabulary.

Then I fell into the routine of my non-challenging job. This job involved ad design, website administration, direct mail campaigns and other marketing tasks. It was pre-Twitter and pre-Instagram—even Facebook was only accessible to those who had college email addresses at the time.

In the winter of 2006–2007, I became fed up with Long Island winters. In yet another snowstorm, my car became encased in ice, and I was unable to open its doors for four days. This was February. Many of the homes listed with the real estate company I worked for were being sold so that the owners could move south. Charlotte and Cary, North Carolina; Austin, Texas; and points further south. During the four-day ice retreat, I researched different cities in the South. I contacted tourism bureaus and signed up for brochures and email updates. By June I knew I wanted to move to Raleigh, North Carolina. I started applying for jobs similar to my current job in public relations or in general marketing. I took phone interviews in my car on lunch breaks. In September, I flew south for three interviews. One turned into a job, and one turned into my first freelance client—although at the time, I didn't realize that freelancing could involve more than a sole client.

After I settled in North Carolina, I started noticing the bios included next to articles in magazines and on websites. I noticed the term "freelance journalist" more often. A few years after my move south, I realized I was still working in marketing for a real estate office—only the geography had changed. In the spring of 2009, I was told my job was secure, but they needed me for only four days per week instead of five. All my benefits remained in place, but my pay shrunk as a result. I used my lunch break that day to visit the library. I wasn't looking for anything in particular, just roaming the stacks and thinking about my pay cut and the extra time I would have on my hands. As I walked past the shelves on writing, a title on freelance writing caught my eye. I checked out a few other books on the business of writing. I couldn't put the books down that night. The more I learned about the feasibility of freelance writing, the more I knew it was exactly what I was looking for.

When I first became interested in freelance journalism in my post-collegiate years, I wrote articles about local places and themes I thought were interesting. I figured it would be easier to connect with a local publication first before reaching out to larger markets. Later I learned this approach is correct, but my method was wrong! Not only did this approach immediately label me as an amateur in the eyes of editors, I was expending time in interviews and writing with no promise of payment. Generally, you pitch an idea to an editor *before* writing the article. Unintentionally, I was doing it backwards.

I point out these rookie efforts and my workflow changes in the stories behind the articles throughout this book. Every article serves multiple lessons and has shaped how I run my writing business today.

Before We Get Started: Why I Wrote This

When I first started learning about freelancing, I found books more helpful than reading advice online. I like to sit and focus, write in the margins, dog-ear pages, take notes and learn what I personally need to get started. I remember how much of a mystery sustainable freelancing was to me, and I considered that feeling while writing this book. If anyone would have visited me back in those first few years living in North Carolina—while I was commuting to a cubicle, feeling sad that my dog was stuck in a crate at home all day and suspecting that I was missing something—this is the book that would have helped me to get to where I am today a little faster.

I often describe my writing business as a three-armed monster:

1. Journalism, my main focus initially, is one arm.
2. Writing search engine-optimized (SEO) web content is another arm, which is what I spend most of my time on as of this writing.
3. Creative writing workshops and classes are the third arm.

Some of the many benefits of freelancing are that you can pick and choose what you work on, change your focus on a whim and evolve with industry demands and your own interests. Journalism might become my main focus again sometime, or I may simply continue pitching articles at my current pace, which is exclusively on what interests me. When I teach classes on freelance journalism, people often tell me it sounds like so much *work*. Yes, it's a *job*, people! You can make it a side job or your full-time focus. Make it work for you.

When journalism was a bigger priority for me, I would send ten query letters every week. Some of the letters were pitching the same article to different markets, and I would move forward with whoever accepted first. If writing and sending ten query letters sounds too intimidating, then start with one.

Reading successful query letters helps writers understand the flow. The letters on their own fall short of explaining the lessons learned behind writing the article and collaborating with a publication. I wanted to gather all of my queries in one place, but I also wanted to share their stories and the experiences that came out of producing each article.

Learn the Lingo

From instructing courses on freelance writing and query letter writing, I am reminded that journalism has a language all its own. To help navigate this book and the publishing industry a little better, here are some terms to become familiar with:

- **Department**—Section of a magazine dedicated to a specific topic (e.g., a travel department in a food magazine or a health department in a retirement magazine).
- **Exclusive**—When a writer pitches an idea and delivers the pitch as an 'exclusive submission' it means that the writer has not shared the idea with any other market.
- **Evergreen**—Articles that are essentially timeless. They can be published any time of the year and don't tie into an event, holiday, or other time-sensitive subject.
- **Kill**—Refers to a publication terminating a piece before it's published. Often a kill fee is involved. Usually the terms of the kill fee stipulate that the market acquires all rights to the piece. Kill fees are notoriously low unless otherwise negotiated. Industry standard is approximately 25 percent of the initial article rate. Before accepting and depositing a kill fee payment, take the time and effort to ensure all the kill fee terms are acceptable to you. Acceptance of payment implies acceptance of the terms—be satisfied with the terms first.
- **Market**—This is the outlet for which you write for. A market can be a magazine, newspaper, website, blog, newsletter, or other medium.
- **Reprint rights**—Writers can get paid for the same article multiple times. For example, a market might acquire one-year print rights the first time an article is published. After a year passes, the writer can pitch the article as a reprint to another market. This offers the writer the opportunity not only to get paid again, but to break into/get a byline in another market.
- **Query**—The pitch letter, often an email, to persuade an editor to accept the article idea and the writer. This book is full of successful queries!
- **POA/POP**—Payment on publication (POP) is industry standard, but writers can negotiate payment on acceptance (POA). With POP,

a writer's payments are mailed or wired when the article hits newsstands or is digitally published. Sometimes articles get pulled or delayed. Writers can negotiate POA to help prevent delay of their payment.

- **Spec**—Writing a piece "on spec" or a "spec piece" means that there is no promise of publication. The editor speculates the piece may be a good fit, but needs to read a draft first before deciding.
- **Syndication**—Some markets offer syndication services. These services provide for automatic distribution of the same article to different markets. Usually the writer gets paid for each market where the article appears.

General Workflow When Writing for a Magazine or Newspaper

Although many variations occur within the article publishing process, the general flow involves conceiving the ideas first. Some writers find that picking a market first helps them develop ideas best suited for the market. Overall, here's how it works:

1. Article Idea
2. Write Query
3. Pick Market
4. Pitch Query
5. Editor Accepts (Verifying Compensation if Not Already Known)
6. Write Piece
7. Submit Article with Invoice
8. Receive Payment

Article Ideas

Writers are often at one end of the spectrum: they either have too many ideas or feel challenged envisioning interesting topics. If you have experience in other areas of writing, namely creative writing, you know how important it is to remain observant. Stories are all around you. Here are a few ways to help generate article ideas:

- **Consider the type of article.** Profiles (of people, places and events), interviews, exposé/investigative journalism, long-form features, blurbs, etc. For example, I wrote a story about dog GPS devices for one magazine. Then I wrote a piece for another magazine profiling the families who rescued their lost dogs as a result of these devices.
- **Who you know.** You likely know specialists in different fields. Ask them what's happening in their industry and what new challenges they are facing.
- **Legislation changes.** Changes in the law have a ripple effect. There are stories of the lawmakers, how the law affects the public, etc.

- **Other articles.** Read! You might read an article in a national magazine and realize you could spin a local angle on it in your area. Alternatively, you may see a small-town story that could be expanded with a national lens. Also, as you read through a magazine that you want to write for, look for other angles you can take on existing articles. When sending your query letter to the editor, you can cite the previous article and how your piece will complement that topic and appeal to their readers.

Write the Query

Queries normally range from 3–4 paragraphs.

- First: your hook.
- Second: optional, to flesh out the idea more.
- Third: title, word count, etc.
- Fourth: you and your relevancy.

A basic query should have a hook in the first paragraph to get the editor's attention. Think of the first paragraph as the beginning of your article, since you will need to hook the reader too. A second paragraph fleshing out more details, statistics, or expert information follows; it is optional and best used in pitches for long features. The third paragraph is the nitty-gritty breakdown of the entire piece: your snazzy title and word count, the section or department it's intended for, or the specific seasonal issue for which it may be most appropriate. Your last paragraph explains why you're the best person to write the piece. Where has your work appeared, what are your credentials—not just your education, but your work/life experience—and have you written on this topic before?

Your query letter is your only chance to catch an editor's eye. You need to sell the article idea and yourself. If you have a personal connection with the editor, mention that in your first line. A personal connection can be anything from hearing them speak at a conference or on a podcast, interacting with something they posted on social media, or meeting them in person.

Pick Market

As noted above, sometimes writers pick a market *before* they develop an idea. When trying to find magazines that publish specific topics, you can do a simple internet search or a brief consultation with *Writer's Market*, MondoTimes.com, or another online magazine directory to help refine your search. Of course, analog options are also available. Visit the magazine section of your book store or library, or explore the racks in airports to discover markets. Many publications are not listed in directories, yet they are active and pay freelance contributors. On the other hand, keep in mind that many magazines fold and that directories may be outdated. Consult with the magazine's website for (hopefully) the most current information.

Factors to consider when picking your market:

- **Relevancy.** Is your article idea relevant to their audience? Even if you wouldn't reflexively match your idea to the theme of the magazine, remember that magazines feature specific departments on different areas. For example, I wrote a luxury travel piece for a national beer magazine, and the piece did not mention any alcoholic beverage.
- **Payment.** *Writer's Market* and other directories often include current per word or per article rates. Following acceptance of your pitch, the editor generally relays the article rate. If they don't, verify it and the deadline prior to starting work on the article. This is the time to establish whether your fee is POP or POA.
- **Reputation.** If this is the first time you're writing for a market, do an internet search for "magazine name+scam" or "magazine name+no pay" and see if there are results of other writers who have had negative experiences with the market. There are also sources available to research markets. WritersWeekly.com runs a Whispers & Warnings section. The American Society of Journalists and Authors maintains a system called Paycheck. It's a members-only resource that is a member-sourced collection of payment histories (including rates, timeliness and no-pay experience) and general overview of the writer's experience collaborating with the editor/market.

Pitch Query: Find Editor Contact Information

You have written your highly convincing and eloquent query letter, and you've researched and selected at least one market to send your query to. Now, who is the best person to receive your letter? The editor-in-chief or managing editor may not be the best person to receive your pitch. Some publications have specific department editors, and they may be more appropriate recipients. There are a few different ways to find a magazine editor's contact details:

- **Market website.** Almost every market's website has a section called Writer Guidelines, Contributor Guidelines, Write For Us, Submission Guidelines, or something similar. Check the main contact page or view the About Us (or equivalent) page to see if the magazine editor's contact information is available there. You may have success looking in the magazine's Media Kit too, depending on the size of the publication.
- **Internet search.** A simple web search of "<magazine name> editor email" may produce results. If you find a name but no email address, you can use it to search at the next bullet…
- **Social media.** LinkedIn and other social platforms might be able to direct you to the editor's email. If necessary, you could send your query letter through a social media platform's direct message system. Another method: If you follow the editor on social media, post a status update and tag them, explaining that you would like to send a query and asking where contributors can find their freelance guidelines.
- ***Writer's Market.*** A new edition of *Writer's Market* is published every year. I have never owned a print copy, but I have subscribed to the online version for more than a decade—and still do as of this writing. This is a great source to consult to learn more about submission guidelines, circulation, readership and rates of freelance acceptance. Editors and staff in the magazine and newspaper publishing world change fairly often, plus magazines fold and new ones launch. I personally opt for the online version of *Writer's Market* because you never know what may have changed after the last print version hit the shelves.
- **Masthead.** If you have a print copy of a magazine or can view an online version, flip through the first few pages and you will discover

the masthead. The publisher, editors, photographers, art directors, contributors and all the editorial staff are listed here. In the past, mastheads were merely a list of titles and names. Many markets have taken a progressive approach and revamped their mastheads to include the email address and/or social media handles of each person.

When it's time to email—and in rare cases nowadays, snail mail—your query letter, do one thing before clicking send: ***Follow the submission guidelines***. As you'll learn from the forthcoming stories about the articles I've written, following the guidelines can help earn an acceptance and prevent your letter from being ignored or instantly rejected before an editor even reads it.

I've sent query letters to some magazines that only accept letters during a certain week every month, and others who only accept queries one month out of the year. Some magazines include specific instructions for how to format your email's subject line. They might require you to write "Query: <Department Name>" or "Query - <Your Name>" or some other variation. If you follow the guidelines, the editor will recognize you as a thoughtful individual who follows directions. Win! As with any professional endeavor that involves selecting the right person, strict submission guidelines are simply a way of weeding out people who may not work well with the market's editorial process. Better to avoid a mismatch from the start, for all parties involved.

Another important factor to consider before sending your query letter is whether or not your pitch is timely. If you're pitching to a four-color glossy magazine, the publisher likely finalizes the art at least a month or two in advance of the print date. That means all the editorial is complete in advance of that.

If you're pitching an article that is not evergreen (see the **Learn the Lingo** section if you're unclear about what this means), count back 4–6 months from the holiday/event that it is tied to. It's important to consider the long editorial process magazines run on when you pitch. You should pitch articles about New Year's resolutions, for instance, in July or August. Pitch features about summer camps in December or January (possibly earlier since enrollment for summer camps often occurs in the spring).

Editor Accepts: Yay!

In most cases, when an editor responds with an acceptance, they explain the rate of compensation and the deadline date. Some publications require a contract, which can be great or a deal-breaker. (See the **Contract Terms to Avoid** section.) It's now your prerogative to either accept or decline the terms. You can also try to negotiate.

To record the terms, reiterate the rate, word count and deadline date in your acceptance email. If the editor has not provided details of a payment schedule, request this information now. For example, simply write: "As we have not worked together before, I look forward to learning more about your payment schedule for contributors. Unless I hear otherwise, I will submit an invoice with my article. Please advise if you require any details from me." If the editor has not provided a formal contract, your email correspondence can help serve as evidence of the work assigned.

If a formal contract is provided, as with any legal document, do not sign it without carefully reading it. If provisions of the contract are unclear, see if a writing organization you belong to has a contract or legal help committee. Of course, there is no substitute for an attorney's review.

Some uncomfortable situations you might encounter regarding payment:

The editor offers a rate less than what they pay other writers. Maybe a writer-friend of yours recently wrote for the same market and submitted a story of approximately the same length. You know they were paid more than what the editor offers you. This is an opportunity to ask the editor two things:

1. Has there been budgetary changes that prevent the market from maintaining the same compensation that has been provided to other writers?
2. Can I submit a shorter article or perhaps include fewer sources—which corresponds to less time for interviews—for the offered rate?

The first question educates the editor that you are very familiar with their market, know at least one other contributor to their publication and have the professionalism to recognize magazine budgets are protean. The second question can help the editor stay within budget while still securing you a byline and ensuring your fee. Another option is to name a higher rate and suggest a longer article, a sidebar or two, supply photos—and maybe video/audio if the market is progressive enough to find digital content valuable.

The editor (or the publication) will not negotiate terms. As you'll learn in the stories behind the articles throughout this book, on at least one occasion, an editor responded to a pitch with an acceptance—but also that their freelance budget was exhausted for the year and that no compensation was available. I declined. In other cases, the negotiation may not be about the rate, but about the legal terms surrounding your work. Indemnity clauses, and the other items noted in the preceding pages, can be deal-breakers if the publication is unwilling to strike or amend the terms.

Steps When an Editor Rejects

Occasionally an editor rejects a pitch and is generous enough to explain why. On more than one occasion, I've received a rejection where the editor said, "Great idea! We ran a piece on that in our current issue, out yesterday." They include a link to the exact piece I had pitched. This is known as the day-late-and-a-dollar-short syndrome.

Generally, though, editors do not respond with a rejection. Consider the volume of pitches they receive while overseeing the day-to-day demands of publishing. They may be writing their own articles too. If you get no response, send a follow-up email. Depending on the timeliness of your pitch, you might send a follow-up a few days or a week later, but usually a two-week window is generous enough—especially for articles that have no pressing time constraints.

If you receive a rejection or you never receive a response from the editor, submit your article elsewhere. If you're really serious, use this as an opportunity to do two things:

1. Re-read your query to see if you can improve the pitch with a revision. It often helps to get an extra set of eyes on the letter. A trusted friend might notice something in it that you can improve.
2. Send your pitch to two more markets. That way, you'll know it's not just under consideration at one market.

Getting Paid

Writers can always negotiate POA in lieu of POP. POP is generally the default and often frustrating for magazine writers. Writers may have to wait months or years between pitching a query and seeing their byline in a four-color glossy. If you're waiting to be POP, that's a long time to postpone your rent or mortgage payment! Simply ask if POA is possible. If not, consider whether or not POP fits your values. If not, withdraw your query, thank the editor and mark that market off your list. Pitch your query elsewhere.

Sometimes a magazine does not pay, even when they say "the check is in the mail." Every writer has a different workflow for how to handle this. Generally, it involves a few frequent emails and a phone call or two to get the matter addressed. If contact with the editor does not resolve the matter, it's time to contact their superior. Beyond this, a certified return receipt letter can also help document your payment demands. If you have a contract or prior emails that provide for when payment is made, cite the payment schedule in the contract or email history.

And, of course, an attorney's counsel may be necessary. Volunteer Lawyers for the Arts is an organization I often recommend in my workshops. VLA offers reduced or free legal services for individuals in creative fields. Connect with VLA, legal advocacy sections of writing organizations, or search for intellectual property attorneys in your area.

I have never pursued small claims court to retrieve payment from a magazine, but some writers take that approach. If this is a situation you find yourself in, consider that some magazines have contracts that stipulate that court proceedings occur in the state where the publication is located—which may be different from where you reside.
While I have never followed the public humiliation approach, and I don't recommend it, I have witnessed other writers who have taken their slow or no-paying magazine to Twitter and other social media platforms and brought the situation to public light. This has ended favorably for some, and not well for others.

If you are not getting paid by a magazine, cease work and decline all future assignments until payment is made in full. If you eventually receive payment, consider whether this is really a market you want to work with again.

Many writing organizations offer payment support, such as sample demand letters, small claims court tips, and links to important legislation protecting freelancers. Some writing organizations may even contact the magazine on your behalf if there is a contract issue. A few to check out are the American Society of Journalists and Authors, the Freelancers Union, National Association of Independent Writers and Editors, National Writers Association, National Writers Union, among many others. A list of these resources, among others, is included in the back of this book.

Liabilities

Journalists are exposed to many risks in their work. Depending on the topic and the scope of the work, some writers are at a greater risk than others. It's important to understand the liabilities so that you can make informed decisions when reading contracts and accepting assignments. I only touch on a few common liabilities below, but there are many others that might target a freelance journalist in a lawsuit and potentially risk loss of their assets. Remember: No information in this book constitutes as legal advice and writers should never make legal decisions based on information that is not provided by a qualified attorney.

Copyright/plagiarism. Some underhanded writers plagiarize work, while others may unintentionally commit plagiarism by failing to properly reference or cite text. Copyright infringement claims could result.

Libel and slander. The main difference between libel and slander is that libel is a written form of defamation/harm and slander is a spoken version. Generally, writers need to be concerned about libel since their work is written, but slander claims are possible if defamation allegations surface about false statements the writer made.

Misappropriation of name/likeness. Writers might neglect to acquire consent to use the name/likeness of a person or entity.

Privacy. Public disclosure of private facts is another area that could be grounds for legal action. Invasion of privacy claims might surface.

Journalists also need to consider that in some cases errors and omissions may be made by the magazine, but that the liability falls on the journalist. For example, a writer may submit their article, but prior to publication the editor might change quotes or facts. Upon publication, sources could be upset and file suit about misquotations, defamation, or any other damage or injury that results as part of the error. Even if the writer is innocent, sometimes litigation is needed to prove that. It also tarnishes the writer's relationship with their sources.

The cost and time involved for court proceedings could be devastating. It's important for writers to be cognizant about risks, vigilant when reading and signing contracts, and informed about media liability insurance that can help cover legal representation.

Contract Terms to Avoid

It is rare that the initial offering of a contract is the most favorable version for a freelance journalist to sign. Negotiations are commonly imperative prior to signing the contract.

Disputes. As noted in an earlier section, some contracts state that any legal disputes will be handled in court within the jurisdiction where the publisher is located. Freelancers may write for markets that are headquartered outside of their state of residence. This could cause a burden should any claims arise.

Indemnification clauses. Indemnity clauses are included in contracts to determine which party holds blame in the event of a lawsuit or claim. If these clauses are present, they are usually not in favor of the writer. The provision often holds the publisher harmless from all claims and places the burden entirely on the freelance writer. In most cases a writer can ask that the clause be removed entirely. In the event that is unacceptable, another option could be to amend the clause so that the writer is only liable for content "as submitted or approved by the writer." (Side note: I had a positive meeting and generous assignment offer from an organization—not listed in this book—that would have increased my annual income by 20 percent. When I received the contract though, it had an indemnity clause that placed all liability on me. I requested the editor amend or remove the clause, and his superiors refused. While the assignments came with little risk, I declined the work due to the legal risk and on the principle that I don't believe markets should place that burden on a contributing writer.)

Misunderstanding rights. Contracts could have clauses for myriad types of rights: audio, copyright, digital, film, moral, print, etc. New writers and even established freelancers often cannot adequately describe moral rights. Research these terms and meet with an attorney to ensure you understand them and how they apply to you.

POP. From the **Learn the Lingo** section, POP means payment on publication. Writers can negotiate payment on acceptance. For example, a provision could be added that states the publisher owes payment to the writer within 30 days of article acceptance, and if not satisfied, the kill fee terms apply.

Rights purchased. It is often in the writer's best interest to request addition or modification of any provisions that pertain to rights and payments. For instance, a magazine publishes an article but does not pay the writer. If the contract included a provision that the magazine only acquires rights upon payment for the work, there is an issue.

Scope of work missing. Ensure that the word count, delivery schedule, topic, payment, allowed expenses, deadline, kill fee, and other basics are included in the contract. In the event the editor requests an expanded article or earlier delivery; the contract can be cited to help protect the writer or negotiate increased compensation or rush delivery fees.

Media Liability Insurance

Media insurance policies are available for writers and others in the media sphere to cover claims of slander, libel, copyright or trademark infringement and other liabilities. As a writer, you can purchase a policy annually to cover writings related to your journalism, writing business, or you can purchase a policy specifically for a book. If you are writing about a celebrity, political figure, or controversial topic, you may want the peace of mind of a media insurance policy. There are a number of insurance companies that provide these services—research them and review with a professional to select the appropriate one for you.

Query Letter Mistakes

Sometimes unintentional actions cause a pitch to be ignored or discarded. In other cases, the writer's perspective or approach prevents them from breaking into new work. Here are a few mistakes to avoid before sending your query:

1. **Not personalizing.** Skip "Dear Editor" and instead do the research to find and personally address your query to the editor by name. Remember, if you have a personal connection (met at a conference, heard on a podcast, etc.), mention it in your opening.
2. **Not following up.** If your piece is time-sensitive, send a follow up email in less than a week. Perhaps your piece is so pressing you might need to follow up the next day. Be courteous and explain your check-in is not intended as a nuisance, but simply hinging on the time-sensitive nature of the article. For less timely pieces, follow-up two weeks later. Your initial query may have simply been lost in the shuffle and a simple follow-up can remind the editor of their interest.
3. **Typos.** Not only should your query letter be free from grammar and punctuation errors, it should reference the correct magazine name. Yes, I'm guilty of this error. I copy/pasted a query that I sent to one magazine and neglected to change the magazine name before I sent it to another market. I've also done that with the editor name too. If you catch your error, send a follow-up email acknowledging and apologizing for the mistake. Sometimes that humility and attention to detail are received well.
4. **Irrelevancy.** Try to avoid pitching a Halloween-themed article to a magazine in early October. As noted earlier, magazines plan their editorial far in advance. A Halloween piece should be pitched in May or June.
5. **Timing.** While there is no official rule for this, I find it's best to avoid sending query letters on Mondays or Fridays, late at night or extremely early in the morning—unless, of course, the submission guidelines tell you to! (Side note: If I plan to send several queries, I will write them in advance and format email drafts. I might write them late at night or on a weekend, not times when I would send them. Then I keep them in my draft folder until an appropriate time to send them.)

6. **Short-sighted newbies.** I was paid as little as $65 for one article. In some of the freelance journalism classes I've taught, some students balked at the low rates of some articles. They asked, "Why would I want to write a query letter for an article that paid so little?" These writers don't look at the big picture, and so they often are not successful as freelancers. Credibility in a new area can be a gateway to higher-paying markets in that field. Sustainable freelancing is often a mix of different streams of income from writing, not from one sole area. In the stories shared in the following pages, I reference other connections I made, article sources, article ideas, speaking gigs, clients, etc. Don't make the mistake of being short-sighted and solely focused on dollar signs.

Ways to Earn More Per Article

An article does not have to be viewed as a single finite income producer. Writers can profit off a single article in several ways, plus there are opportunities to increase compensation for an article.

1. **Awards.** This is a two-sided approach. One, writers can submit their article for annual journalism awards. Some of these awards have monetary compensation. Even if they don't, including that you're an award-winning journalist in your future query letters can help in negotiating higher rates. Two, if you have received an award in a specific area and pitch an article on that topic, mention that in your query letter. You might be able to leverage that award and your credibility when negotiating your article rate.
2. **Book.** Sometimes a feature-length article proves to be inadequate as a storytelling platform. Or, a writer has amassed many clips on a particular topic that it becomes evident a book-length medium is in order. Columnists often publish collections of their work in book form, and some journalists become so passionate about a topic after writing an article on it that they decide to write a book about it. A big bonus: If you are a journalist who writes successful query letters, it will likely be much easier for you to write a query letter to an agent for your book.
3. **Movie.** As noted in the prior bullet, sometimes a medium is inadequate for a certain story. A documentary or a film inspired by an article could be another means of earning income and authority.
4. **Expertise/specialize.** If there is a specific niche you intend to carve out for yourself, seek certifications and education that can help make you more attractive to editors. In the same vein, if you're trying to establish credibility in a certain area, pitch and write articles in that field. If you become known as a women's health writer, it's easier for editors to recognize you and assign work, leading to more income over time. Specializing in certain topics makes writing about those matters easier over time, which can help reduce the amount of time needed for researching and finding sources.
5. **Syndication.** Syndication services allow a writer to be paid multiple times for the same article, often earning a fee for each market where the article appears.

6. **Photos/media.** Invest in a professional camera and photo editing software. If you're unsure how to best use the tools, invest in photography classes and take a photo editing course. You'll see in some stories behind the query letters included in this book that when I offered complementing media with the article I was able to negotiate higher compensation.
7. **Sidebars.** Suggest the possibility for side bars in your query letter. Instead of pitching an article about how to start your own vineyard, pitch an article on that topic with a sidebar of wine schools and academies, food and beverage classes, and higher education programs in hospitality. If it's a regional publication, be sure to name drop a few in the area.
8. **Speaking gigs.** If you're trying to start or grow income from professional speaking, consider pitching articles on topics related to those that you present at speaking gigs. The articles can help boost your credibility with event planners when they choose speakers. (And if you have a book related to your articles and speaking topics, usually these events are prime places to sell your book.) Also, if relevant to the article you're pitching, include a note in your query letter that you regularly speak on the topic and reference a few notable gigs.
9. **Writing projects.** If you want to grow your income through other forms of writing (web content, content marketing, brochures, speeches, etc.), having your byline under topics that are relevant to these areas can help attract the right clientele. For instance, as a journalist I've written for a handful of agricultural publications. As of this writing, one of my areas of specialization for my content marketing writing clients is agriculture. When I work with food growers they recognize my journalism experience and it sets me apart from other content writers.

Non-Financial Benefits of Bylines

It's not just about the money. Sometimes intangible benefits are more attractive to writers. For one, journalism can help establish oneself as an expert in a specific field or fields. This helps build credibility, makes the pitching process "easier," and allows you to repurpose your contacts—basically saving you time when trying to find sources.

For business professionals, writing for magazines can help increase authority among clients or customers, make them more memorable among peers for referrals, and help differentiate themselves from their competition.

Developing bylines in specific niches can also create avenues for guest spots on radio shows, podcasts, and on TV. Media producers in these fields need to fill the air with stories and having a journalist on for a special segment helps them accomplish this.

For journalists who are interested in writing books through traditional publication—via literary agent representation)—bylines in magazines are often attractive to agents. A writer with a history of journalism credits shows a literary agent that the writer produces publishable material, can work with editors, and has ways of reaching new readers. Sometimes literary agents 'discover' writers because of an article they wrote.

Journalists also acquire translatable skills that they can tap for the rest of their professional careers, no matter which direction their respective career takes. Storytelling, research, interview methods, collaboration, revision – all of these skills can make the writer more valuable in other fields.

Articles can also help writers educate and inform the public on causes and organizations that they care about. Sometimes this is more valuable to the writer than the payment.

Templates to Jumpstart Your Workflow

Here are a few templates I've developed over the past seven years that I now use whenever I start a new article.

Article Template

I find a "sandwich" approach helps me produce an article if I'm on a time crunch. I write the opening and the closing of the article, then it helps me fill in the space in between.

Opening: Consider using the hook from your query letter as the opening for the article. Alternatively, choose two things that surprised you when you started interviewing sources and researching the article. Consider these two items and your query letter hook, and pick the best one for your opening.

Closing: During your interviews with sources, note quotes that stand out. They may make for a strong closing line. Other option: Write down the two main points you want the reader to be left with and then decide which one of those would end the story on the right note. A third option: Decide how you can tie an element from your opening into the end to bring the piece full circle.

When delivering the article, ask the editor if they have a particular template that they require. Sometimes markets provide a template where they want sources, pull quotes, and the article body placed to make it easier for their layout department to manage. When a publication has no particular needs, this is how I deliver the file:

SOURCES:
Name, Title, Phone, Email, Address
Name, Title, Phone, Email, Address
Name, Title, Phone, Email, Address
Article title:
Subtitle:
Byline:
Word Count/Side Bar Word Count:
Sidebar: (if any)
Article:
Bio: (if the publication prints one)

Interview Template

Time and again I learn that writing the article usually requires the least amount of time. Conducting interviews is the biggest time demand. To help manage and respect your time and that of your sources, use a template as a base, set a time expectation/limit for phone or in-person interviews and consider whether an email interview would be adequate for your needs. (In some circumstances, you don't want to interrupt the flow of a good interview – so be prepared.) Here's my template:

BASICS
Name/How they want their name to appear:
Title/Occupation:
Years of experience in this field:
Notable degrees:
Phone:
Email:
Mailing Address:
CUSTOM QUESTIONS
3-5 questions

Depending on the topic, I usually have 3-5 questions that I know will help me move forward with the article. Sometimes the conversation prompts other questions naturally. Expect to shift focus.

As with any journalistic efforts, ask open-ended questions. *How* and *Why* are ideally the best ways to start questions as they limit the terse yes/no or one-word responses. Questions are not always required in an interview. You can also request more information on a topic. Sometimes mentioning an issue or matter and then asking the source to tell you more about it is another way to keep the interview valuable. (Side note: Sometimes interviewees request to see the questions in advance. It's up to you whether you want to provide this. For the work I do, I find it a helpful courtesy.)

I used a digital recorder to document interviews before I had a smartphone. There are many phone applications that allow for simple recording of calls or in-person interviews. (Although I have not found any that I have been happy with or recommend.)

Be mindful of the laws that pertain to recording calls. These laws vary by state and sometimes require that you disclose on the call that a recording device is being used. All parties on the call might be required to agree/consent to the recording. This is usually of greater interest to journalists who are involved with investigative journalism as they might not want their subject to be aware of the recording device. Not only do laws vary by state, they also vary based on where each party is located. For instance, some states do not require disclosure of the recording if the originating party is in a different state than the party they are calling. This can usually be documented naturally by commenting on the weather. Small talk about the weather allows the recording to show where each party is located for the call. As with any legal matter, consult an attorney to learn the laws in your state.

Thank You Letter Template

I am a big promoter of thank you letters, particularly handwritten ones. Whenever possible, I try to enclose a hard copy of the article (or entire magazine) in my thank you letter. If I send via email, I include a link to the article. I try to send thank you letters as soon as the piece is published. The sources are often eager to see their name and quotes in print, and it helps maintain a positive relationship with them in case I need to call on them for future articles. Here's my template:

Dear NAME:

Thank you for your time and insight for my piece in MAGAZINE. I enjoyed our discussion and learning about TOPIC, especially THIS PARTICULAR TOPIC. I'm really proud of the article and glad we connected. If you or someone you know is involved with anything related to TOPIC, please let me know. I'm always interested in potential story ideas. I'll be in touch in the future if I work on another piece that requires your input.

Thanks again,
Tara Lynne

Get Started Now

If you've ever read a successful query letter, you understand the basic flow of the letter, but when you read many successful queries in one sitting, you understand the formula much faster. It's an iterative process that feeds on repetition.

When I meet people who are interested in writing for a living, especially for magazines, I stress that it's a constant process. If you decide today you want to professionally write for magazines, that means you probably won't get paid until about six months from now—assuming your article idea is accepted. Every week, you need to send queries out so that there's always something in the pipeline.

For example, I pitched an article idea to America's favorite beer magazine, *Draft*, on June 7, 2011. The editor responded and accepted the article topic on August 31, 2011. Tick, tock… that's 2 1/2 months. The article was due in December and slated for their special travel-themed issue. On March 27, 2012, I received a check and a copy of the magazine featuring my article. Tick, tock… that's 7 months after my query was approved and 9 1/2 months since I sent the original query!

So, if you're interested in writing for magazines: Do it now. What are you waiting for?

All My Magazine and Newspaper Query Letters That Worked for Me

All of my successful query letters to date—from 2009–2017—are alphabetized by market name and then sequentially by date for articles in the same market.

Back Home Magazine

(FYI: This publication went out of print in 2014.)

Initial Query: Unverified. (I switched email addresses around this time and I cannot determine the actual date.)
Accepted: February 2011
Published: March 2011
Paid: February 2011
Fee: $75
Word Count: 800 words, approximately
Idea:

An event about backyard chicken ownership was held near where I lived, and a friend had invited me to go. The man leading the presentation mentioned a lot of interesting things about chickens. He touched on training chickens, composting and gardening with chickens and the possibilities of increasing the nutritional quality of egg production. My family had backyard chickens when I was growing up, so I have a long connection with raising poultry. Even though it had been many years since I had first-hand experience with chickens, it was surprising to hear concepts that were new to me.
The instructor helped found and participates in an annual event in the Raleigh area called the Tour d'Coop. It is held to increase awareness of the benefits of backyard chicken ownership and helps support a local faith-based organization.

Sources:

The instructor of the backyard chicken workshop I attended had a few connections. I also met homeowners with backyard flocks on the Tour d'Coop. I live in close proximity to the North Carolina State University Veterinary School, so I reached out to poultry scientists there who had completed or observed studies on chicken diets and egg nutrition.

Query:

What if you could increase the nutritional value of your eggs from backyard chickens? Researchers have shown it is possible to alter chickens' diets and offer them special care to lower cholesterol and increase Vitamin D and omega-3 fatty acid content. Simple adjustments like supporting a vegetarian diet, adding canola oil to feed and providing a free-range lifestyle show great health benefits.

"The Good Egg" will be approximately 800 words and feature insight from poultry experts, backyard chicken owners and poultry veterinarians.

Interested in this piece in *Back Home Magazine*? I'm available to discuss your ideas and thoughts. I'm a freelance writer based out of Raleigh, North Carolina, with publication credits in AirTran Airways' *GO Magazine, GRIT, Triangle Gardener* and work forthcoming in *Produce Business*. You may learn more about my work and view clips at www.taralynnegroth.com.

Let me know if you have any questions about this story idea. Thank you in advance for your time and consideration.

Bay State Parent

Initial Query: March 2011
Accepted: April 2011
Published: May 2011
Paid: June 2011
Fee: $25 (reprint rights)
Word Count: 1,000

Idea:

I had a reminder set in my calendar for when the rights to my *Chesapeake Family* story would become available again. Once the time had passed, I started pitching reprint rights to other parenting/family-oriented magazines. I decided to pitch the idea for spring publication because a lot of parents generally make their children's summer camp plans then. This article would help them find funding and make decisions about their child's wellness and summer. The editor at *BSP* asked me to adjust the article with a New England focus. Minor adjustments didn't take long.

Sources:

See ***Chesapeake Family*** for the original article's information. For the reprint, the editor connected me with camps in the magazine's distribution area.

Query:
Parents searching for a teen weight loss camp have a difficult time turning over their credit card after they see the $5,000+ tuition rates, some are even priced at $1,000 just for one weekend. Parents may not realize that the tuition is not a bill, it's an investment in their child's life with immense returns. Also, since weight loss camps only came into existence during the past few decades, many are not aware of the numerous opportunities available to offset the cost of this investment.

"Easy Ways to Pay For Weight Loss Camp" is approximately 860 words. It focuses on tax-savings tips through flex accounts, qualifications needed for health insurance reimbursement, the often-unknown loan opportunities available through behavioral health finance originators and scholarships. The article includes advice from financial planners and insurance experts.

Interested in reprinting this piece in your "Camps" section or as a feature in *Bay State Parent Magazine*? Last winter, it appeared in *Chesapeake Family*, a regional publication. I am available to discuss your ideas and thoughts. I am a full-time freelance writer residing in Cary, North Carolina, and have written for *GO* (AirTran Airways' inflight magazine) and *Southern Neighbor*, and I have work forthcoming in *Back Home Magazine*. You are welcome to view clips at www.taralynnegroth.com.

Let me know if you have any questions about this story idea. Thank you in advance for your time and consideration.

Blue Ridge Country

Initial Query: March 2011
Accepted: March 2011
Published: September 2013 (Yes, this date is not an error!)
Paid: November 2013
Fee: $100
Word Count: 460

Idea:

In 2009, I drove from Raleigh, North Carolina to Manchester, Tennessee to attend the Bonnaroo Music Festival. I also wrote the first guidebook to the festival that year, which I took out of print in 2016 due to lack of time to keep it updated. On my way to Bonnaroo, I planned to stop at a few places. After a little bit of online searching, I had settled on one of the spots: The Lost Sea. As described in the query below, it's a lake in a cave. While touring the cave, I learned from the guide that they hold overnight camping trips for Boy Scouts and other groups. It seemed like a unique experience, one that requires different preparation than traditional above-ground camping. I had pitched the idea of profiling cave camping to other publications, but it was regularly turned down. Then in March 2011, I received an invitation from the editor of *Blue Ridge Country* for article submissions.

Then you might notice the time gap. The initial turnaround time for the article was fairly quick. My pitch was accepted in March, then I sent the finished piece in April. Then, crickets. In September 2013, I got a "blast from the past" email—literally, the editor wrote that in the subject line—and he said they still held the piece on file and wanted to use it as exclusive content for their new digital edition. He wanted to make it more media-rich since it would be digitally featured, so we scheduled a short call to discuss ideas.

Sources:

I referred to formal organizations like the United States Geological Survey and regional speleological societies to connect with relevant sources. Many of my other sources were indirectly linked to the subject of a separate article I had written (see ***Chapel Hill News***) profiling a mountain climber. I posted on social media that I was looking for people with experience spending time overnight in a cave, particularly those with quality photos and videos. The climber responded to my post and got me in touch with a wonderful and active listserv for a cave club in our region. I received a half dozen responses. Finding quality cave photos and video is tough! The listserv was a big help, though. To minimize my time searching for media, I asked my assistant at the time to handle it. She made connections, organized the photos and sent them along.

Query:

Hike below the earth's surface into a cave that once served as the local "Cavern Tavern," an underground bar where moonshine flowed. Float in a glass-bottom boat in America's largest underground lake; view the chamber where the Cherokee tribes held their rituals and see Civil War soldiers' signatures on cave walls. All of this is possible just 3 hours east of Nashville in Sweetwater, Tennessee.

The Lost Sea is a 4.5 acre lake in the Craighead Caverns system. Divers explored the cave in 2005 and discovered a separate chamber. Although today's sonar is still unable to read the actual dimensions due to the sheer size and volume of the cave structure, it is estimated to be approximately 9 acres. For those who aren't afraid of a "bottomless" lake and the dark, camping overnight in the cave system is an adventure easily accomplished in a single weekend trip from Nashville. "Cave-in to Adventure" will be approximately 350 words. What's it like to spend a night in a cave? Are there bats or other animals already living there? What happens if power is lost? These questions will be answered and quotations from the United States Geological Survey (USGS) and caving experts will be included.

Interested in this piece for an upcoming "Country Roads" section of *Blue Ridge Country*? I am available to discuss your ideas and thoughts. I am a full-time freelance writer (and outdoor enthusiast) residing in Cary, North Carolina. My work has appeared in *GO* (Airtran Airways' inflight magazine), *Blue Ridge Outdoors* and *Southern Neighbor*. You are welcome to view clips at www.taralynnegroth.com.

Let me know if you have any questions about this story idea. Thank you in advance for your time.

Blue Ridge Outdoors

Initial Query: June 2010
Accepted: June 2010
Published: September 2010
Paid: October 2010
Fee: $250
Word Count: 1,000, approximately
Idea:

Not long before the time I pitched this article, I had been on a night kayaking event with a planetarium. Morehead Planetarium in Chapel Hill, North Carolina partners with a local paddle outfitter to hold stargazing sessions on a lake. I wrote a separate article about that—see ***Southern Neighbor***. In May 2010, I had been freelancing part-time for a year. I had told myself that if I met all my financial goals throughout the year, I would resign from my job and focus entirely on freelancing. That May, I went on my last paid vacation (to Paris), and on the day I returned to work, I gave my boss my letter of resignation, which included 6-weeks' notice. I worked in a small office and there was no pressing need for me to jump ship on the traditional 2-week timeframe. My job had been stress-free and the owners were kind, so I wanted to be generous in giving notice and transitioning my replacement.

Once the owners selected my replacement, I began training her. She was curious about the work I was doing that had prompted me to leave the job, so I explained my freelance writing work to her. The next day, she brought in a copy of *Blue Ridge Outdoors*, a regional magazine. After looking over the latest edition and their website, I thought that my night kayaking experience would fit well with their editorial. I pitched an article about prepping for nighttime kayaking, but the editor preferred a personal encounter. I accepted. To get the experience fresh in my mind, I went out on the water at night again, but this time on a moonless night, on a river instead of a lake and on an outing unrelated to the planetarium's trips.

Sources:

Since this was a personal perspective piece, I was the source. Although I did chat with the staff of the outfitter for some quotes.

Query:

A paddle can be just a paddle unless you visit some place new—or just visit during a different time—at night. Paddlers can experience new fun with their existing kayaks through night paddling. Night kayaking delivers a new level of excitement as one can see and hear different things.

"Top Tips for a Night Paddle" will be approximately 1,000 words and include photos. It will bring a new dimension to the typical expectations that surround a kayak trip. Safety tips involving efficient lighting and navigation will be covered. It will feature advice from established paddling outfitters and kayakers and outline simple safety steps to make the most of a unique and memorable experience.

Interested in this piece for an upcoming issue of *Blue Ridge Outdoors*? I am available to discuss your ideas and thoughts. I am a freelance writer residing in Cary, North Carolina whose work has appeared in *Southern Neighbor* and the *Providence Journal*, and I have work forthcoming in *Back Home Magazine*. You are welcome to view clips at www.taralynnegroth.com.

Let me know if you have any questions about this story idea; I look forward to hearing from you soon. Thank you in advance for your time.

Blue Ridge Outdoors

Initial Query: None. Editor offered assignment after my article above.
Accepted: n/a
Published: October 2010
Paid: August 2010
Fee: $200
Word Count: 1,000 words, approximately
Idea:

After I submitted my article about night kayaking, the editor invited me to write a profile about a few marathons taking place around the same time in the Baltimore, Maryland, area that were all celebrating notable anniversaries.

Sources:

The editor connected me with a few long-time marathon runners. They were all accessible and a joy to chat with.

Query:

Not needed!

Blue Ridge Outdoors

Initial Query: December 2010
Accepted: December 2010
Published: February 2011
Paid: March 2011
Fee: $100
Word Count: 500 words, approximately
Idea:

My friends regularly traveled to Hot Springs, North Carolina and always extolled the town and the water. Whenever they returned from a weekend in Hot Springs, their chatter circled around the healing properties of the springs, how rejuvenated they felt and plans for their next visit. I had read Bill Bryson's *A Walk in the Woods* and had learned from the book, as well as my friends' tales, that this tiny town was the first stop in civilization for north-bound Appalachian Trail hikers. I had stopped in the town for lunch on my drive to the Bonnaroo Music Festival in June 2010, so the feel of the town was fairly fresh in my mind. After a little online research, I discovered there was another Hot Springs across the state line in Virginia. I thought the proximity of both springs, the hiking connection and the season would be a good blend for an article. (Side note: It wasn't until the fall of 2012 that my now-husband and I ventured to the springs in Western North Carolina and experienced the hot water firsthand. A treat!)

Sources:
At the time I was working on this article, I was active in a local rock climbing group. I figured a few of the members must have experience hiking the AT or at least knew others who did. I asked the group's organizer to send a note asking for AT hikers who had stopped in Hot Springs to get in touch with me. What happened next spurred another article.

One of the rock climbing group members responded to my note. He had recent experience hiking the AT and visiting Hot Springs. Perfect! However, he was just about to leave the country for a nearly month-long climb to benefit a local charity. See ***Durham News*** for the story about that article.

Query:

Winter hiking, snow camping and skiing can leave people exhausted, sore and cold. Outdoor enthusiasts can heat things up before spring thaw with a winter visit to hot mineral baths in the mountains of North Carolina and Virginia. Hot Springs, NC, is a staple stop for Appalachian Trail thru- and section-hikers, as well as rock climbers. Alternatively, Hot Springs, VA (adjacent to Warm Springs), has been host to Thomas Jefferson, thus naming their waters Jefferson Pools. The naturally hot waters in Jefferson Pools have been flowing for almost 10,000 years and today boast the merit of being the oldest spa in the United States. 150 miles of hiking trails stretch the area.

"Get Hot in the Cold" will be approximately 1,000 words and include photos. It will explore the lodging options, AT trail tips, note unique hiking spots and outline the health benefits of the mineral waters. Winter adventurers will learn the highlights about these relaxing destinations to complement a strenuous visit outdoors.

With most AT thru-hikers beginning their journey in March/April, interested in this piece for a February/March issue of *Blue Ridge Outdoors*?

Blue Ridge Outdoors

Initial Query: March 2011
Accepted: March 2011
Published: May 2011
Paid: June 2011
Fee: $100
Word Count: 600 words, approximately

Idea:

Since my night kayaking experience had spun off into multiple articles, I thought of other outdoor activities that could take place at night. The experience of doing something that may be commonplace or adventurous during the day takes on a new and different appeal at night. A few zip lining facilities were opening across the state, and many were already established. I saw that some offered zip lining at night. When I sent the query below, the editor explained they had just run a piece on zip lining and didn't want to run anything in a similar vein the next issues. However, he needed someone to write a piece about sports massage. I accepted!

Sources:

The editor supplied all the sources I needed.

Query:

Note: Although this query turned into a different story, I can repurpose it with a different market.

In a similar vein to the night paddling article from last September, there is a nocturnal twist available on weekends for zip liners just north of Asheville. Whizzing from tree to tree illuminated only by lamplight and starlight, nighttime canopy tours in the mountains of Western North Carolina are bringing outdoor enthusiasts not only a bird's eye perspective of the wild, but an experience of another kind of "night life."

"Night Life on High" will be approximately 800 words. It will bring readers a peek at how zip lining at night can be more exhilarating with a greater need for safety. Advice on what zip liners should do to prepare for a nighttime adventure, additional gear required and what sights and sounds are a part of the adventure will be included.

Interested in this piece for a June or July issue of *Blue Ridge Outdoors*? Looking forward to hearing your thoughts.

Chapel Hill News

(published via *News & Observer*)
Initial Query: December 2013
Accepted: December 2013
Published: February 2014
Paid: March 2014
Fee: $125
Word Count: 800
Idea:

Bartholomew Barker (www.bartbarker.net) is one of the poets who co-organizes Living Poetry (www.livingpoetry.net) with me. Bart invited me and the other group organizers to his mother's art exhibit—an art exhibit you had to touch to experience. His mother creates art for the visually impaired. Her pieces had exhibited around the country and in England a few times; this time, they were going to be on display in Hillsborough, North Carolina, not far from Chapel Hill.

There was a short time between when I learned about the exhibit and when the show started, so I knew I had to pitch to a local newspaper. (Although I think her art would photograph beautifully in a four-color glossy spread!) Since I already had a connection with a local paper from a previous article (see ***Durham News***), I figured I would pitch the idea to the editor there first. Like the time before, the pitch was accepted the same day I made it.

Sources:

Bart connected me with his mother, the artist.

Query:

The blind are not able to see works of art like "Starry, Starry Night" or the "Mona Lisa," but they can experience masterpieces from art history through a touchable art sequence opening soon in the Triangle.

Hillsborough-based artist Sarah Barker created homages to works of art from some of the greats such as Picasso, Da Vinci, van Gogh and Warhol. Her "Tactile Color" exhibit travels across the country showing how a fabric-centric color wheel system, which Barker created called the B-code, allows visually impaired people to "see" art through touch. Barker quilted specific textures to create touchable versions of famous art pieces. Experiencing such iconic art by touch brings a visually impaired person's connection with the piece to a deeper level. Her traveling exhibit opens at the Hillsborough campus of Durham Technical Community College in January 2014.

"Art for the Blind" will be approximately 800 words. It will explain how Barker developed the B-code system and how the exhibit is the first of its kind to bring art, which was once only visually consumed, to a new audience. Photos will be available.

Interested in this piece as a feature or as a profile in *The Chapel Hill News*? I am available to discuss your ideas and thoughts. Since my last piece for *The Durham News* a few years ago, I've published articles in *Blue Ridge Country* and *Deep South*. You may view clips at www.taralynnegroth.com.

Thank you in advance for your time; I look forward to hearing from you soon.

Chesapeake Family

Initial Query: November 2009
Accepted: December 2009
Published: January 2010
Paid: January 2010
Fee: $100
Word Count: 1,000 words, approximately
Idea:

Outside of my journalism work, I also write web content and provide content marketing for businesses. One of my clients was a weight loss camp for teenagers. I wrote the camp's newsletter, press releases, social media updates and some of the web content. I became familiar with the consumer perspectives of parents and children. Also, childhood obesity was just beginning to be discussed and addressed seriously. At the time, First Lady Michelle Obama made awareness and prevention of childhood obesity a prime focus of her efforts. I knew magazines are busy in the winter slating their spring and summer content, so I thought an article in a parenting-focused magazine about weight loss summer camp options would fit well.

In correspondence with the editor, we decided a better angle would be chronicling and explaining the various ways of covering the costs of a summer at weight loss camp. A short time at camp could cost several thousand dollars—and, as noted in my article, some weekend stays are $1,000. Parents would likely need to pay for the cost of child care for the balance of the summer before and after camp takes place.

Scholarships, payment plans, crowdfunding and other sources could help offset or completely cover tuition—and not all parents are aware of these options.

Sources:

A simple internet search led me to funding sources, loan providers and health insurance companies with programs tailored to covering weight loss efforts.

Query:

Heart disease in their thirties, arteries of 45-year-olds—these are characteristics of one in six children, and more are at risk. According to reports released earlier this year by the Centers for Disease Control and a recent article by CNN's John Blake, most children today are obese, and they're not aware of the lifestyle changes available to maintain a healthy weight.

"Best Weight Loss Options for Kids and Teens" will be approximately 800 words. It will focus on the opportunities parents can explore with their children—such as restrictive diets, gastric bypass surgery, weight loss camps and change of lifestyle. The piece will include expert advice from certified nutritionists, weight loss camp directors and former campers from around the Southeast.

Interested in this piece as a feature in *Chesapeake Family*? I am available to discuss your ideas and thoughts. I am a freelance writer residing in Morrisville, North Carolina who has written about weight loss camp options for Suite101.com. My work has also appeared in *Southern Neighbor, The Stony Brook Press* and the *Providence Journal.* You are welcome to view clips at www.taralynnegroth.com.

Let me know if you have any questions about this story idea; I look forward to hearing from you soon. Thank you in advance for your time.

Dad's Divorce

Initial Query: March 2011
Accepted: March 2011
Published: May 2011
Paid: May 2011
Fee: $100
Word Count: 1,000, approximately (market turned the piece into 2 pieces)
Idea:

In the summer of 2010, I separated from my then-husband. When tax season rolled around, I received an automatic email from a popular online tax filing service, alerting me that my password had been changed. Before I could attempt to retrieve the password, I received another alert that the email address associated with the service's account had been changed—to my soon-to-be-ex-husband's email address. He and I had filed our taxes jointly once, the prior year, through my account.

I immediately contacted customer service associated with the account and explained what happened. They asked me if I was still married. In North Carolina—and this is still true as of the writing of this book—archaic legislation prevents married couples from filing for divorce until they have been physically separated for one year and one day. At the time this tax fiasco occurred, I was still 6–7 months away from the date I'd be legally permitted to file a complaint for divorce with the county clerk. If I could have filed sooner, I would have! I relayed all of this to customer service, and their apathetic response was that since we were still legally married on paper, he was entitled to access the account, even though it was registered to me.

Media coverage at the time had focused on stories about illegal or unauthorized online account access and identity theft. Some broadcasts I heard and watched, and articles I read, explained that this type of access, particularly identify theft, may qualify as a criminal charge. I lived less than a mile from a police station, so I drove over there and asked to speak to an officer. After explaining the situation, the officer told me the same thing: My soon-to-be-ex was still legally my husband, so he was not committing a crime; however, if he had violated the Terms of Use of the service, there could be charges. Since the tax service had told me there was no problem, I faced a dead end.

I decided this was an important matter that most individuals navigating divorce were likely unaware of, and so this was worthy of an article. I asked the tax service how I could prevent this from happening again. I asked the police officer the same. I found other sources, as noted below, to help identify ways that would make it virtually impossible for spouses or significant others to (easily) access accounts that are not their own.

Sources:

The local police station and an online tax service were initial references. Then Help a Reporter Out helped connect me with mortgage brokers and other divorcing or divorced individuals who had experienced similar violations to mine.

Query:

Your mother's maiden name. The name of your first pet. The city where you were born. These are all ubiquitous security questions used by email providers, online shopping sites and financial institutions. What happens when you're divorcing and the person you shared your life with—who knows the answers to these questions—uses this information to hack into your personal accounts, email, maybe even steal your identity?

"Divorce and Identity: New Security Measures" will be approximately 1,000 words. It will focus on identity theft laws, what hackers are accountable for and how accounts and finances can be protected as a marriage is dissolving. The piece will encourage alternative security options, identity theft insurance and credit vigilance. Advice from financial service advisors, law enforcement professionals and attorneys will also be included.

Interested in this piece as a feature for *Dad's Divorce*? I am a full-time freelance writer residing in Cary, North Carolina; my work has appeared in places such as *GO* (AirTran Airways' inflight magazine), the *Providence Journal* and *Chesapeake Family*. I also hold a bachelor's degree in cultural studies and keep a strong pulse on trend shifts. You are welcome to view clips at www.taralynnegroth.com.

Dad's Divorce

Initial Query: May 2011
Accepted: May 2011
Published: June 2011
Paid: June 2011
Fee: $100
Word Count: 1,000 words, approximately

Idea:

As noted in the last query letter, I was navigating divorce at the time I pitched this article. One of the issues that came up in the early months of the separation was custody of my dog. Fortunately, North Carolina law (as is the case in many states) treats dogs as property. I had waited until I owned a home before I got a dog. Less than a week after closing on a home, I went to a local animal shelter. I met my dog then and officially adopted him a few days later. Fortunately, the dog (my property) was acquired more than a month before my marriage. No custody disputes were possible. That is not the case for many other couples, and I thought this area would make for interesting editorial.
Sources:

An Internet search helped connect me with family law attorneys and divorce lawyers. Also, the husband of a writer in my critique group is a divorce lawyer, and I was able to interview him as well. Help a Reporter Out connected me with authors of books on divorce law and mediators.

Query:

Thank you for your payment for my divorce and identity security piece. When time allows, I'd love to get your feedback on another article idea for DadsDivorce.com:

Childcare and custody arrangements are top priorities for divorcing parents. What about family pets? Who is responsible for vet bills, food costs and care for a family dog? According to 2011 reports from the American Pet Products Association, Americans' pet care spending is over $54 billion. With dogs and cats treated like members of the family in most homes, and children's attachments to their pets being strong, conflicts can arise over where cats and dogs should reside.

"In the Doghouse—Where Does Fido Go?" will be approximately 1,000 words and provide fathers the latest statutes on canine and feline custody. Budget alternatives and custody scenarios will be presented and recommended. Quotes will be provided from attorneys and divorced pet owners.

I look forward to hearing from you soon. Thank you in advance for your time.

Dad's Divorce

Initial Query: Editor assigned July 2011.
Accepted: July 2011
Published: August 2011
Paid: August 2011
Fee: $75
Word Count: 982
Idea:

By this point, I had regularly written and delivered a few articles to the editor. At month's end, the editor noticed he had a surplus in his freelance budget. Although it was less than the standard article rate, he offered the extra budget to me first. I had free reign over the topic, and since they had never requested revisions and I had a lot of unused quotes and notes from my other interviews, it was painless and not too time-intensive to come up with a quick article. I sent the two-line pitch below and delivered it three days later, ahead of schedule.

Sources:

I used the sources from previous articles, plus I met writers in my poetry groups who had been through divorces. Some had represented themselves and others had hired attorneys.

Query:

How does an article about the risks and losses of a DIY divorce sound? It will feature loss of property ownership, reduced custody rights and the greater expense of securing counsel after taking the DIY route.

Dad's Divorce

Initial Query: August 2011
Accepted: August 2011
Published: September 2011
Paid: September 2011
Fee: $100
Word Count: 980
Idea:

Glenn, one of the writers in Living Poetry, the poetry group I co-organize, saw some of the articles I had written for *Dad's Divorce* on my Facebook profile. He thought that exploring the respectable timeframe that single parents should consider before introducing their child (or children) to a new partner would make a good article. He suggested the idea, and we had a solid chat about how it would appeal to the large single-parent demographic.

Sources:
I had developed reliable sources through the last few articles I wrote for this market. I tapped a few of those, plus made a new call for individuals on Help a Reporter Out.

Query:

When time allows, I'd love to get your thoughts on another article idea. I'm interested in writing a piece about appropriate timelines for introducing dad's new girlfriend to children. Should there be a 6-month rule, should an ex-wife grant approval first? Psychological and social aspects will be explored through advice from certified counselors and behavior specialists.

Looking forward to hearing your thoughts.

Deep South Magazine

Initial Query: February 2011
Accepted: February 2011
Published: April 2011
Paid: May 2011
Fee: $100
Word Count: 1,048
Idea:

As described in a few other stories included here behind my query letters, I attended the Bonnaroo Music Festival in Tennessee in the summer of 2010. Later that year, I published the first unofficial guidebook to the festival. As part of book marketing efforts, I wanted to pitch and publish articles related to or complementing music festivals, ideally articles that would publish in the months prior to the festival, which is held annually in June.

As you'll notice below in the query, my pitch is focused exclusively on the Bonnaroo Music Festival, but my published article does not take such a concentrated approach. Instead, when the editor responded to my query, she asked if I could instead pen the piece addressing musical festivals in the South. That seemed logical to me—and would likely be read by more people—so I agreed. The editor also offered to run a giveaway of my book, which was quite a helpful offer!

Sources:

From researching and writing my Bonnaroo guidebook, I learned about many music festivals in the surrounding area. I picked a handful of festivals and reached out to the organizing teams. I interviewed festival administrators to help give first-time and veteran festival-goers tips on ways to maximize the comfort of their experience at a music festival during the summer heat in the South.

Query:

What does one wear to a four-day camping music festival on a 700-acre farm under the Tennessee summer sun? The Bonnaroo Music & Arts Festival attracts 100,000 music lovers each June, and the crowds get sweaty and dusty. Plus, no one wants to see a hippie in a fanny pack. To be able to make the most of the music festival experience and enjoy the community and music, comfortable and fashionable festival attire is best planned in advance.

Music festival-goers can experience a higher level of comfort by taking advantage of the latest innovations in festival fashion. Wallets disguised as wrist bands mean less to carry around in the heat, plus with pearl and patterned designs, women can enjoy stylish flare. Bonnaroo is notorious for mud, and although young women may desire boho-chic gladiator sandals, waterproof boots are a popular sight throughout the festival grounds. However, there are new boots specifically designed for festival attendees that convert the heat created by the wearer's feet into electricity to recharge cell phones.

"The Best of Fest Fashion" will be approximately 1,000 words and will detail accessories for men and women that are fashionable, festival-friendly and reminiscent of the hippie generation. They make a festival attendee's experience more comfortable and stylish. Interviews with the fashion creators and music festival veterans will be included. A sidebar of music festivals around the southeast will also be included.

Interested in this piece for the May/June issue of *Deep South*? I am the author of *How Do You Roo? A Survivor's Pocket Guide to Bonnaroo*, the first—and currently only—guidebook for the Bonnaroo Music & Arts Festival. As a full-time freelance writer residing in Cary, North Carolina, my work has appeared in places such as *GO* (AirTran Airways' inflight magazine), *Blue Ridge Outdoors* and *Chesapeake Family*. You are welcome to view clips at www.taralynnegroth.com.

Let me know if you have any questions about this idea. I look forward to hearing from you. Thank you in advance for your time and consideration.

Dog Fancy

(This magazine changed its name to *Dogster Magazine* in 2015.)
Initial Query: February 2010
Accepted: May 2011
Published: October 2011
Paid: November 2011
Fee: $550
Word Count: 1,008 words (article), 270 words (side bar)
Idea:

My dog was quite the escape artist. His repeated escapes prompted me to research solutions, and I learned that new products allowed for remote tracking of dogs. The systems varied in price and features, and I noticed the big canine-related magazines had yet to publish a current piece about these devices. If you take a look at the dates above, you'll notice one year and eight months passed from when I originally pitched the article until when I was paid.

At the time I pitched to *Dog Fancy*, the magazine had specific submission guidelines. They only accepted queries during a limited time of the year, and they planned their editorial far in advance. I didn't hear back after that pitch period, so I continued pitching the same idea elsewhere. Then I wrote an article about the various types of GPS devices for dogs that was published in *FIDO Friendly* in October 2010. (See ***FIDO Friendly***.)

My experience at this point working with editors was limited to email only. To my surprise, while I was walking on the streets of Boston (while I was in the city for a stop on my book tour for the Bonnaroo guidebook), I got a phone call from an out-of-area number. If I don't recognize the number, I generally don't answer the call. I received a voicemail from the editor of *Dog Fancy*, and he wanted to move forward with my GPS pitch. When I got back to my computer, I had also received an email from him. This was an especially pleasant surprise because I had changed my website and my email address. I'm glad at least my phone number remained the same—but I was happy knowing the editor took the extra step to find me.

We scheduled a time to talk, and he explained they were interested in an angle geared more toward the successful rescue stories that occurred as a direct result of using a dog GPS device. I agreed, and explained that angle worked well since I had published the article about the technology aspects in *FIDO Friendly*.

Sources:

I tapped my sources from my *FIDO Friendly* article to see if there were individuals or families willing to share their rescue stories. I also posted a call on Help a Reporter Out. This connected me with new GPS devices I had not heard of before, plus families and dog owners who—in some cases, repeatedly—found their lost dogs with the assistance of GPS devices.

Query:

A runaway dog, while in a familiar neighborhood or on vacation, is a stressful event. What if your dog is pregnant, needs medicine or has a hearing impairment? Even a healthy dog runs the risk of a car accident. Very few dog owners take advantage of an affordable luxury that helps limit the amount of time a beloved canine is lost: a GPS tracking system for dogs.

"Hot on Their Tail: GPS For Your Dog" will be approximately 1,200 words. It will review options for GPS tracking systems for dogs, share experiences of reunited dogs and owners and encourage a modern twist on responsible dog ownership. It will also include advice from veterinarians about which breeds are more prone to run away or "escape."

Interested in this piece as a feature for *Dog Fancy*? I am available to discuss your ideas and thoughts. I am a freelance writer residing in Cary, North Carolina who has been published in *Dog Living Magazine* and has work forthcoming in *FIDO Friendly Magazine*. You are welcome to view clips at my site www.taralynnegroth.com. Please be advised this is an exclusive submission.

Let me know if you have any questions about this story idea; I look forward to hearing from you soon. Thank you in advance for your time.

Dog Living

Initial Query: April/May 2009, approximately (I switched email addresses a few years later and cannot determine the actual date.)
Accepted: April/May 2009, approximately
Published: November 2009
Paid: n/a
Fee: None.
Word Count: 653
Idea:

I discovered this magazine when I picked up a free copy at a local store. I was interested in writing about canine topics, but had no clips in that realm. After I contacted the editor for contributor guidelines, I learned that the magazine did not pay contributors. I also learned the articles were not terribly long or in-depth. Since I was just starting out, I decided to write a piece for no pay, strictly for the byline in a four-color glossy canine-related market. I figured this small sacrifice would help open doors for paid work down the road. Plus, I could always sell reprint rights. When I inquired, the editor explained they take exclusive rights for one year. After this piece was published, I marked a note on my calendar for the following year to start pitching reprint rights. (See ***FIDO Friendly*** for that story.)

Sources:

I interviewed the vet I had at the time.

Query:

It's bedtime. Don't forget to brush Rover's teeth before he goes to sleep! Dogs are not resistant to cavities and canine dental work can be pricy. Most dog owners are lax about brushing their dog's teeth and don't realize how effective this inexpensive preventative action is for their pet's health.

"How Important Is Brushing Your Dog's Teeth?" will be approximately 650 words. It focuses on the benefits of canine dental health on the rest of the body, how brushing your dog's teeth should be a priority for dog owners and how toothpaste for humans differs from formulas designed for dogs.

Interested in this piece for *Dog Living Magazine*? I am available to discuss your ideas and thoughts. I am a freelance writer residing in Cary, North Carolina who has published work in the *Providence Journal* and *Stony Brook Press,* and I have work forthcoming in *Southern Neighbor*. You are welcome to view clips of my work at www.taralynnegroth.com. (I am also an owner of an Australian Shepherd-mix who loves having his teeth brushed every evening!)

Let me know if you have any questions about this article; I look forward to hearing from you soon. Thank you in advance for your time.

Draft

Initial Query: June 2011
Accepted: August 2011
Published: February 2012
Paid: March 2012
Fee: $200
Word Count: 300

Idea:

One of the trend-spotting services I subscribe to, Springwise, had a blurb about floating hotel concepts. No, not cruises, but hotels that floated and could move from port to port. These concepts had highly futuristic designs. I went to Barnes & Noble and explored the magazine racks. I picked a few to flip through and noticed *Draft* (self-described as "America's Favorite Beer Magazine") had a travel section. (Notice that I specifically reference the department by name in my query below.) Upon researching the contributor guidelines, I learned they were particularly interested in items about luxury travel trends.

Sources:

I contacted the companies developing these floating hotel concepts. These were international companies, so the language barrier was a slight issue. Patience and Skype helped bring the interviews to fruition.

Query:

Sweden's Ice Hotel made headlines in the 1990s. The bizarre seasonal structure attracts guests with the experience of staying in a hotel made completely of snow and ice. With the onset of climate change, the hospitality industry is stepping ahead with floating hotels. If sea levels may rise, why not grow the wow-factor of hotels' destination experiences?

Resembling a biodome, the Remistudio Ark Hotel is a luxury hospitality concept currently in the works. The floating structure will be heated by natural light and energized by wind turbines and solar energy. The hotel will also be tidal wave-resistant and completely safe from other natural disasters. Another developing concept by MORPHotel revolves around a luxury experience where the floating hotel changes shapes. Unlike a cruise ship where guests may suffer seasickness from rough seas, the MORPHotel has been designed to change its shape based on environmental conditions.

"Check In and Float On" will be approximately 350 words. It will deliver readers the latest floating hospitality concepts, what stage the development processes are in and what to expect from a floating hotel experience. The piece will feature insight from architects and hospitality professionals.

Interested in this piece for the "On Tap Life" section in an upcoming issue of *Draft*? I am available to discuss your ideas and thoughts. I am a full-time freelance writer residing in Cary, North Carolina who keeps a strong pulse on industry trends. My piece following the hospitality trend of night classes offered at hotels around the country appeared in *GO* last fall. My work has appeared and is forthcoming in *GRIT* and *Blue Ridge Outdoors*. You may view clips at www.taralynnegroth.com.

Let me know if you have any questions about this story idea; I look forward to hearing from you soon. Thank you in advance for your time.

Durham News

(co-published in *The Chapel Hill News* via *News & Observer*)

Initial Query: January 2011
Accepted: January 2011
Published: February 2011
Paid: February 2011
Fee: $100
Word Count: 800
Idea:
I met the subject of this article when I was active with an indoor rock climbing group. I interviewed him for a different article (see ***Blue Ridge Outdoors***, "Get Hot in the Cold") and during our talk, he mentioned he was planning to participate in a benefit climb of the highest summit in the Western hemisphere. The donations for his climb would benefit a nonprofit organization in Durham. Since the climb was taking place rather soon and it involved a local individual doing something extraordinary that would benefit a local organization, I pitched a local newspaper.

Although my pitch was accepted on the same day I made it, the story shifted. The climber was in a remote area with no communication available and not set return for nearly three weeks. I arranged a deadline with the editor after the climber's return. When the climber got "back on the grid," I learned that he had suffered from altitude illness that prevented him from completing the climb. Was the story gone? Would I burn a bridge with an editor the first time I worked with him? No and no. While the climber himself couldn't finish the climb and had recuperated under medical care at a lower elevation, others in his group continued on. Also, pledges for his climb exceeded his $10,000 goal by $2,000. A story of perseverance and personal sacrifice remained, and the story ran.

One thing that was different about this article than any other I'd written is that the editor asked me to come to the paper's office in person to review some article details prior to publication. This was the only time as a freelance journalist that I'd been asked to do this. I don't recall the specific details discussed, but I remember they were minor and could have probably been clarified via a short phone call. I remember it took me longer to find a parking space—thank you, downtown Chapel Hill!—than I spent visiting with the editor.

I've written a few articles that generated a rush of public comments and inquiries. This is one of the articles that stand out in that regard. I received several emails from readers telling me how much they enjoyed the story. Writers know how good it feels to hear positive feedback from readers, but it's particularly rewarding to know readers took time to track down my contact information to send me their feedback.

Sources:

I met the climber via an indoor rock climbing Meetup group. He had helped connect me with cave campers for another article I wrote (see ***Blue Ridge Country***). I also interviewed the director of the nonprofit the climb benefited.

Query:

On the day after Christmas, when most people traveled and kids played with new toys, Durham resident Mark Daughtridge flew to Argentina, where he began a three-week expedition to the summit of the highest mountain in the Americas, Aconcagua in the Andes Mountains. He will be raising $1 for every foot he travels, which will be used toward improving the Durham community.

Daughtridge, an outdoors enthusiast with rock climbing and alpine hiking experience, was inspired to raise funds for the Religious Coalition for a Nonviolent Durham through this adventure because of his own personal experience. Ten years ago, Daughtridge was a victim to a break-in in his house; the reconciliation program available through the coalition helped him re-establish his home. Today, the coalition assists victims of crime by covering rent and bills for victims' families.

"A Long Climb from Durham" will be approximately 1,000 words. It will give readers an inside look at a local outdoor enthusiast's adventure, what type of training he's conditioned himself with (like weekly trips to the North Carolina mountains carrying 60 lb. packs), detail how the Coalition for a Nonviolent Durham has been helping the community recently and what plans they have for the future. Photos will be available as well.

Interested in this piece for an upcoming issue of the *The Durham News*? I am available to discuss your ideas and thoughts. I am a freelance writer residing in Cary, and my work has appeared in *GO* (Airtran Airways' inflight magazine), *Blue Ridge Outdoors* and the *Providence Journal.* You are welcome to view clips at www.taralynnegroth.com.

Let me know if you have any questions about this story idea; I look forward to hearing from you soon. Thank you in advance for your time.

FIDO Friendly

Initial Query: Unverified. (This also was around the time I switched email addresses. If I were to make an educated guess, I probably sent the query letter in March or April since I knew the reprint rights were becoming available.)
Accepted: Unverified. Likely March or April as noted above.
Published: July 2010
Paid: May 2010
Fee: $65.00 (reprint)
Word Count: 650
Idea:

I originally wrote a piece about canine dental health for *Dog Living Magazine*, a regional publication for dog lovers in the Carolinas. It was later reprinted in *FIDO Friendly*.

Sources:

I interviewed my veterinarian at the time.

Query:

It's bedtime. Don't forget to brush Rover's teeth before he goes to sleep! Dogs are not resistant to cavities and canine dental work can be pricy. Most dog owners are lax about brushing their dog's teeth and don't realize how effective this inexpensive preventative action is for their pet's health.

"How Important Is Brushing Your Dog's Teeth?" is approximately 650 words. It focuses on the importance of canine dental health on the rest of the body, how brushing your dog's teeth should be a priority for dog owners and how toothpaste for humans differs from formulas designed for dogs.

Interested in reprinting this piece for your "Health and Wellness" section in *FIDO Friendly Magazine*? Last fall, it appeared in *Dog Living Magazine*, a Carolina regional publication. I am available to discuss your ideas and thoughts. I am a freelance writer residing in Cary, North Carolina who has also had work published in *Southern Neighbor* and *Chesapeake Family Magazine*. You are welcome to view clips of my work at www.taralynnegroth.com. (I am also an owner of an Australian Shepherd-mix who loves having his teeth brushed every evening!)

Let me know if you have any questions about this article and if you would like to review it; I look forward to hearing from you soon. Thank you in advance for your time.

FIDO Friendly

Initial Query: May 2010
Accepted: June 2010
Published: October 2010
Paid: September 2010
Fee: $68
Word Count: 680
Idea:

Around the time I pitched this article, I moved out of my townhome and into an apartment. Neither living space had a fenced yard, and my dog was almost two years old—still very much a puppy. He was adept at squeezing past my legs anytime the front door opened, and when he was on his leash, a standard collar was insufficient for keeping him tethered. When researching online for solutions, I came across GPS devices for dogs, a relatively new concept then. I was pitching the idea to different canine magazines, but once I got my foot in the door with *FIDO Friendly* for the reprint of my canine dental health article, pitching the GPS idea was well received. If you look at the timeline between these two articles for *FIDO Friendly*, you'll notice I waited until I was paid before I pitched my next article—an important rule to follow!

Sources:

I contacted the product manufacturers of the GPS devices. Some companies helped connect me with individuals responsible for conceiving of and designing the products, while others provided easy-to-access and responsive marketing departments.

Query:

Note: This is essentially the same pitch I made to Dog Fancy *(see the story behind* **Dog Fancy** *to learn why).*

A runaway dog, while in a familiar neighborhood or on vacation, is a stressful event. What if your dog is pregnant, needs medicine or has a hearing impairment? Even a healthy dog runs the risk of a car accident. Very few dog owners take advantage of an affordable luxury that helps limit the amount of time a beloved canine is lost: a GPS tracking system for dogs.

"Hot on Their Tail: GPS for Your Dog" will be approximately 1,200 words. It will review options for GPS tracking systems for dogs, share experiences of reunited dogs and owners and encourage a modern twist on responsible dog ownership. It will also include advice from veterinarians about which breeds are more prone to run away or "escape."

Interested in this piece as a feature for *FIDO Friendly*? I am available to discuss your ideas and thoughts.

Let me know if you have any questions about this story idea; I look forward to hearing from you soon. Thank you in advance for your time.

GO

(AirTran Airways' inflight magazine, *GO* was named 2009's Best Inflight Magazine by North American Travel Journalists Association. It ceased publication when AirTran merged with Southwest Airlines in 2014.)
Initial Query: March 2010
Accepted: August 2010
Published: November 2010
Paid: September 2010
Fee: $550
Word Count: 800 approximately (article), 500 approximately (sidebar)
Idea:

This is yet another feature I can attribute to Springwise, the trend-watching service. I read about cultural classes and theatrical events for guests at a Seattle hotel. After a quick internet search, I learned other hotels had created "voluntourism" and other unique programs to give travelers a more intimate experience with local culture than they would normally get at a standard hotel. I had been trying to break into the inflight market because I knew the rates were a bit better, so I decided to use this angle as a pitch to *GO*. *GO*'s writer guidelines requested that queries only be sent during one week each month so that the editor could present new ideas to editorial staff at a monthly planning meeting. I hadn't received an email declining or affirming my query, so a few months later, I started implementing a follow-up process. I'm glad I did! The editor responded within a day or two and, if memory serves me correctly, had just wrapped up the meeting and the idea was well-received.

The turnaround for delivery was fairly quick. I had less than a month to prepare the article, which means finding and contacting sources, scheduling interviews, and all the normal journalistic administration. I learned *many* things from writing this article that shaped my approach to all the articles that followed this one:

1. Always follow up. I can't say for sure that the editor would have accepted my article if I had not followed up on my pitch, but it certainly didn't hurt my cause.

2. Set a precedence and time limit for interviews. This is very difficult, as you don't want to be rude *and* you don't want to cut off or prevent your subject from delivering a great quote. I recorded hour-long interviews with nearly every subject for this article. Plus, when I had to do revisions, I needed to schedule additional interviews.
3. When writing for inflight magazines, only reference locations where the airline flies into. In my initial draft of the article, I had 2–3 items in the sidebar for cities that AirTran didn't even fly to. My amateur experience with inflight markets showed brightly then!

Overall, this article was a huge time suck. Five revisions were required, more than any other feature I've ever written. If you calculated my paid fee by the hours that I spent working on this article, it would be pennies per hour. In the introduction of this book, I have a section (see **Query Letter Mistakes**) dedicated to novice freelancers who scoff at low pay rates. This is a great example of looking at the big picture. This article had a great rate, but in the end, it really wasn't a great rate for the amount of work it took. This article's overall time commitment was mainly a result of my own novice experience writing for paid markets and lack of experience writing for inflight markets.

If you look at the timeline of my freelance journalism you see that my first *paid* piece was only one year before this one. Much of freelance journalism is learning by doing. This book, and no book, can be a substitute for that. If I had read a book like this *before* pitching my first inflight market, I'm confident my experience would have been more positive!

An important rule to follow when citing your education: I rarely mention my degree in query letters. My B.A. is in cinema and cultural studies. When I pitch film-related articles, I say I have a degree in cinema; when I pitch social/cultural pieces, I say I have a degree in cultural studies. Only if I pitch a business or finance piece do I mention that I have six years of residential and commercial real estate experience and that I'm a former licensed real estate agent. Otherwise, it's non-essential. Think about your own experience in this light.

Sources:

Reporter Connection and Help a Reporter Out helped me find business travelers who had taken advantage of the programs featured in the article or similar programs. For the hotels, I contacted each one individually and reached out to marketing and/or the directors of the respective programs.

Query:

Travelling from city-to-city and spending days in business meetings leaves little opportunity for experiencing a region's culture. A new trend in the hospitality industry is delivering guests local and artistic luxuries through "night school" programs conveniently located within the guests' hotel.

These programs bring an interactive and educational twist to a hotel stay by hosting musicians, writers, mixologists and theater casts. Guests can talk with authors and discuss book readings and learn about history and preparation of cocktails, as well as speak with local actors about their craft. Travelers won't have to put their lives on hold when traveling for business with this new trend. Downtown Seattle's Sorrento Hotel began providing this service to their affluent guests, and other hotels such as The Mandarin in Miami and the Four Seasons in Scottsdale offer gourmet cooking classes for hotel guests.

"Corporate by Day, Culture by Night" will be approximately 1,200 words. It will bring readers into a new shift in hotel offerings so that they may have better experiences on their business travels with more control over their work-life balance. The piece will feature insight from hotel managers' and travelers' experiences.

Interested in this piece for *GO*? I am available to discuss your ideas and thoughts. I am a freelance writer residing in Raleigh, North Carolina with a B.A. in cultural studies who keeps a strong pulse on industry trends. My work has appeared in the *Providence Journal* and *Chesapeake Family*; I also have work forthcoming in *Blue Ridge Outdoors*. You are welcome to view clips at www.taralynnegroth.com.

Let me know if you have any questions about this story idea; I look forward to hearing from you soon. Thank you in advance for your time.

GRIT

Initial Query: August 2010
Accepted: August 2010
Published: May/June 2011
Paid: April 2011
Fee: $300
Word Count: 800 words, approximately
Idea:

A homeopathic physician in Raleigh had reached out to me about several health benefits she was witnessing among patients who were consuming raw camel milk. She made broad claims about camel milk consumption completely eliminating autistic behaviors in children with autism who drank it daily. She wouldn't connect me with these patients or their families, so there were no means for me to validate the claims. Instead, from what I learned about the health benefits of raw camel milk and the pending federal regulations for camel dairies, I thought those in agriculture would be interested in the story and future opportunities with expanding dairy businesses.

Sources:

A local physician who contacted me with the story idea connected me with a camel dairy farmer in Amish country. I located other camel owners through Reporter Connection and the Help a Reporter Out network. The North Carolina State University Veterinary School was a good contact for finding an expert on camel milk.

Query:

Goat farms and alpaca farms are in the agricultural vernacular, but camel farms? For the first time in the United States' history, a burgeoning cottage industry is forming around camel milk, which touts dozens of healthy properties like low cholesterol and high vitamin content. It has shown to be beneficial for diabetics and autistic children. Reuters reported last month that the European Union is expected to grant export approval in 2011, which will bring camel milk to the US market. Consumers will be looking for more cost-effective options outside of imports; there are approximately a dozen camel farms in the US awaiting the Food and Drug Administration's approval for commercial sales.

"10 Things You Need to Know About Camel Farming" will be approximately 1,500 words. It will bring readers the important details about camel feed, care and breeding. Facts such as 1 in 4 camels are stillborn will be delivered alongside details about climate, which camels are extremely versatile to (farms have started in Amish country in Pennsylvania to southwestern climes in Arizona). The piece will feature insight from camel farmers and camel milk researchers.

Interested in this piece as a feature in an upcoming issue of *GRIT*? I am available to discuss your ideas and thoughts. I am a freelance writer residing in Cary, North Carolina who keeps a strong pulse on agricultural trends. My work has appeared in the *Providence Journal* and *Chesapeake Family*; I also have work forthcoming in *Back Home Magazine* and *GO*, AirTran Airways' inflight magazine. You are welcome to view clips at www.taralynnegroth.com.

Let me know if you have any questions about this story idea; I look forward to hearing from you soon. Thank you in advance for your time.

GRIT

Initial Query: April 2011
Accepted: May 2011
Published: January/February 2012
Paid: December 2011
Fee: $300
Word Count: 800 words, approximately
Idea:

One of the trend-focused newsletters I subscribe to, Springwise, piqued my interest about an agro-focused social media platform. Then, when I was interviewing a farmer for another article, he mentioned an organization in his area that was developing a social media service for farmers. After a little online searching, I noticed these services were on the verge in many places. Then I searched *GRIT*'s archive and noticed they had not covered it yet —so I reached out to them with the pitch below.

Sources:

I simply used the contact forms on the social media services for farmers to get in touch with the operators. The farmer I mention above connected me with the service in his area. I was unable to use all of the services I learned about in the article as space was limited. This will be a good topic to revisit in the future to see how long-term growth has shaped agricultural marketing.

Query:

Hope this finds you well. Thank you for your payment and sending along copies of my camel dairy piece. When time allows, I'd love to get your feedback on another article idea for the "Gazette" section:

Websites like Eggzy, which locates local chicken farmers, and Veggie Trader, which connects buyers with their area's locally-sourced produce providers, are bringing a digital edge to agriculture. Along the same vein is the recent launch of Farmbook, a site dedicated to connecting farmers with buyers on an international level. Modeled after Facebook's ease of use, Farmbook is meant to be a connection for all aspects of agriculture on a localized level. From timber, livestock feed and equipment to produce, eggs and meats, every aspect is covered so that users anywhere can connect with those in their own backyard.

"Grow Offline and Go Online" will be approximately 800 words and provide farmers the latest Internet avenues for connecting with customers on a local level. Site costs and features will be outlined and quotes will be included from site creators and users.

I look forward to hearing from you soon. Thank you in advance for your time.

INDY Week

Initial Query: October 2015
Accepted: January 2016
Published: January 2016
Date Paid: February 2016 article, March 2016 photos
Fee: $160 article, $30 photos
Word Count: 800, approximately

Idea:

I live in Pittsboro, North Carolina, a currently small town south of Chapel Hill. (I say "currently" because one of the largest planned developments in the state's history has been approved and is under construction as of this writing.) During Pittsboro's Fall Festival in October, my husband and I stopped in the tool store above The Woodwright's School, a woodworking school made iconic by the legendary craftsman Roy Underhill on PBS. Ed oversees the tool store, and he told us that he had been contacted by a film production crew over the summer. The film crew needed hand tools that would be relevant to a specific era and commonly found in a part of the United States at that time in history. It was for a film starring Leonardo DiCaprio titled *The Revenant*, set to release on Christmas Day. I thought this story would be good for a local publication.

Timing this story had a few possibilities regarding a publication date:

- Just prior to the film's release
- At the film's release
- When Oscar nominations are announced in early January (the film would likely be—and was—nominated for Academy Awards)
- Before or following the Oscars in February

I pitched the story to a local paper and a local magazine, since one would have a more immediate publication date and the latter would be farther in the future. The local paper was not interested. The magazine had exhausted its freelance budget for the year; if I was willing to write the piece for free, there would be space for it. I was not. I pitched it again to the managing editor of another local paper, *INDY Week*, but did not hear back.

Then I was contacted by *INDY Week*'s arts editor around the time of the film's release. He had come across my blog WriteNaked.net and enjoyed a few of my posts. He invited me to submit story ideas should any ever come up. I forwarded along the same pitch, and he accepted.

The piece would be a short post on the paper's blog. The turnaround was fairly short, but nothing unmanageable. While I prepared the story, however, a different piece dropped from the paper, and the editor asked me if I could extend the article and submit it sooner for print.

Since the tool store is close to home, I interviewed Ed in his shop and took pictures of him with similar tools to those he had shipped off for the film's production.

Sources:

I knew Ed from visits to the tool store. Ed gave me the contact information for his contact on the film, and I scheduled a phone call with the film's set decorator. The day after I interviewed the set decorator, he and his colleague were nominated for an Academy Award for their work on the film!

Query:

As Oscar season approaches, Chatham County will have a small space in Hollywood. *The Revenant*, a December 2015 release by director Alejandro Gonzalez Inarritu starring Leonardo DiCaprio and Tom Hardy, will feature props from Pittsboro's The Woodright's School Tool Store. The set design team with Los Angeles-based New Regency Pictures contacted tool store manager Ed Lebetkin and requested his expertise and selection of hand tools used during the 1820s, which is when *The Revenant* takes place.

The film was inspired by real-life events and follows the journey of a hunter abandoned in the wilderness by his hunting team after surviving a bear mauling. The production company sought out an expert on wood hand tools and consulted with The Woodright's School.

Ed Lebetkin manages an inventory of thousands of antique hand tools for woodworking, sourcing pieces from estates, auctions, and private sales all over the country. He is quick to identify the purpose, era and often the exact family responsible for creating each tool. He selected a range of tools likely used during the 1820s that the production crew purchased and used in the film. The Woodright's School is a space from Roy Underhill, the force behind "The Woodwright's Shop," the longest-running show in PBS' history.

"Pittsboro Goes to Hollywood" will be approximately 1,000 words and include quotes from Ed Lebetkin and the film production crew. It will explain which tools were selected for the film and why.

Interested in this for your "Culture" section or as a feature? *The Revenant* releases on December 25, 2015, and the 2016 Academy Awards are on February 28. Perhaps an issue publishing between those dates? I am available to discuss your thoughts. I am a full-time freelance writer based in Pittsboro and a former student of The Woodwright's School. My work has appeared in *The Chapel Hill News, Blue Ridge Outdoors, Southern Neighbor* and more. I hold a bachelor's degree in cinema. There is more information available in my market inventory www.taralynnegroth.com.

Let me know if you have any questions about this idea; I look forward to hearing from you soon. Thank you in advance for your time and consideration.

INDY Week

Initial Query: January 2016 (I followed up in February and April when more details became available.)
Accepted: January 2016
Published: May 2016
Paid: May 2016
Fee: $150
Word Count: 600, approximately

Idea:

In September 2015, I co-facilitated a creative writing workshop that uses aromas from essential oils as writing prompts. It was not the first time I had held a workshop using this format, but it was the first time I held the class in my little town of Pittsboro, North Carolina. It was also the first time I met Barbara Hengstenberg, an artist registered for the class. The class was structured for any creative person, not just writers. Barbara mentioned she had just moved to the area and was invited by the local Parks and Recreation Department to paint a piano for downtown Pittsboro. I didn't think our town could be more adorable, but then Barbara told me about the painted street piano and my skepticism dissolved. She planned to spend the fall and winter painting the piano and then the Parks Department would haul it back to display in town. I thought a story about the town's inaugural street piano would be a good fit for a local paper. After my first piece for *INDY Week* was published in early January, I followed up with the pitch below.

Sources:

I contacted the artist herself and the local Parks and Recreation Department. The Parks Department was able to get me in touch with the family who donated the piano.

Query:

Street pianos have been placed in cities all around the world. They invite community play, and many reflect the culture and personality of a place by using the piano as a canvas. Murals on the piano tell stories about the history and people of the area. This past winter, Chatham County resident Angela Crisp-Sears donated a piano to the Pittsboro Parks Department for this purpose.

The Parks Department selected artist Barbara Hengstenberg, a new Pittsboro resident who has a fresh perspective of the town. A year has not even passed since her relocation from Connecticut, and she's already built strong connections with the creative community across North Carolina. She is the new booking manager for North Carolina Indie-folk musician Paleface, launched a not-for-profit network for artists that supports charities (www.wildesart.com) and has free reign of the piano mural as painter of Pittsboro's first street piano project. The piano is currently painted white and garaged at Hengstenberg's home. She is in the early stages of planning the design, with an anticipated completion date in late spring. When finished, the piano will be kept directly in front of Pittsboro Toys and will remain there until the elements take over.

"Play Time: Pittsboro Street Piano" will be approximately 800 words and explain the piano donor's intentions for contributing the instrument to the town, profile artist Barbara Hengstenberg on her mural design choices and explain the town's hopes for this forthcoming impermanent fixture. Disclaimer: I met Barbara when she took one of my creative writing classes last year. I am coordinating a summer class for artists and writers with her. Just want you to be aware in case you feel that is a conflict of interest.

Look forward to hearing your thoughts.

INDY Week

Initial Query: January 2016
Accepted: January 2016
Published: February 2016
Paid: February 2016
Fee: $120
Word Count: 600, approximately

Idea:

I took a letterpress printing class in Durham, North Carolina, in the spring of 2015. (Note: Take a letterpress class if you ever have the opportunity!) I subscribed to the owner's email newsletter and read in one about a special Valentine's weekend class. Just before Christmas in 2015, I attended a holiday market in Saxapahaw, North Carolina, and discovered a blacksmith who creates, among many iron items, stunning roses. He had commented how popular they are around Valentine's and that stayed in the back of my mind. (Full disclosure: I ordered one of his entwined double hearts as a housewarming gift for my parents' new house.) Around the time I received the email about the letterpress class, I also received an email newsletter from an arts space just one town over from where I live. The newsletter had an invitation to a Valentine's pottery class.

I thought the combination of all these unique romantic alternatives to a ho-hum-wine-and-dine Valentine's would be of interest to a local publication. Since time was of the essence, magazines were not an ideal spot to query. That left newspapers. Being that I had just wrapped up an article for *INDY*, I decided to pitch them. The pitch was accepted the next day and due less than a week later.

Sources:

I directly contacted each of the artisans referenced in the query. I already had contact details for two of the sources and found the other through a simple internet search.

Query:

Greeting card aisles saturated in pinks and reds. Special menus with inflated prices. Roses that wilt and find fate in the trash. Instead of a traditional dinner out and a dozen roses, why not be creative for Valentine's Day? Being that Durham was ranked as one of the Top 10 Cities for Creatives by *Business Insider*, the area demands original experiences.

Durham artisan printer Brian Allen offers a letterpress printing class for couples on Valentine's Day. The class is structured around wood type printing on over a century-old iron hand press, which he suggests couples can use to "print sweet words to each other." Chatham County artist and sculptor Chana Meeks leads a Shape and Design class for creating a clay serving platter. The class is held on the unofficial "Valentine's Eve" at the North Carolina Arts Incubator in Siler City. Couples can work together to create a memorable design, etch their names and notes in the platter, and use it for future Valentine dinners and other holidays to come. And the dozen roses? Opt for one that lasts. Saxapahaw-based Haw River Forge creates custom steel roses.

"For the Creative Valentine" will be approximately 800 words and detail the Triangle's artistic alternatives to a cookie-cutter Valentine's date.

Kraze

(Ceased publication in 2015.)

Initial Query: April 2011
Accepted: April 2011
Published: Summer 2011
Paid: June 2011
Fee: $179.46 (The odd price is a result of the price of two copies of the magazine and postage that were deducted from my fee.)
Word Count: 997
Idea:

I read about a highly refined online dating service in one of my Springwise weekly emails. Then I read about another one in a following Springwise update. These services were connecting people based on a major, specific common interest. This was at a time before Tinder and specialized dating apps existed. I cannot remember where I learned about *Kraze*, but I read somewhere at the time that they were a new publication. I figured since they were new, they would be looking for editorial. I was right. They were easy to write for, with no revisions requested, and quick turnaround. The only reason I didn't write for them again was that I had to pay for clips and the postage to mail them to me.

Sources:

I knew a social media marketing expert through my writing group, so I tapped her for a quote. Through LinkedIn, I learned an old friend and fellow alumna of Stony Brook University had become a social media marketer and consultant, so I connected with her for a quote too. I visited the websites of a few of the dating services referenced in the article and got in touch with the founders or directors.

Query:

Match and eHarmony are nothing new; in fact, online dating may be just as passé as speed dating. They're becoming the "old" dating norms. We live in such a fragmented culture that we need more options to find a person who complements our character. Enter the next generation of matchmaking: Dating 3.0.

Sites are popping up that tap into the specialized needs of our tech-savvy culture. Dating profiles of 140 characters or less, dates matched by DNA, speed dating online using a webcam for 1-minute dates—these are all services offered by websites channeling the immediacy and customization prevalent in our society. Other new sites revolve around love of literature, matching partners based on their favorite books, and a love for music, matching individuals based on the bands they like. Recent statistics show an approximately 20% increase occurred in the past year of dates matched through electronic means.

"Dating 3.0" will be approximately 800 words and will detail the latest innovations in a new wave of online dating. Privacy, lifestyle and convenience will be explored for each dating service. The piece will offer a look into the future of matchmaking and provide hip alternatives to the veteran sites like Match and eHarmony that are now commonplace in online dating vernacular. Interviews with dating site creators and users will also be included.

Interested in this piece for your "Relationships" or "Real-life/Reality" sections or as a feature in *Kraze*? I am a full-time freelance writer residing in Cary, North Carolina; my work has appeared in places such as *GO* (AirTran Airways' inflight magazine) and SheKnows.com. I have work forthcoming in *Dad's Divorce*. I also hold a bachelor's degree in cultural studies and keep a strong pulse on trend shifts. You are welcome to view clips at www.taralynnegroth.com.

Let me know if you have any questions about this idea. I look forward to hearing from you. Thank you in advance for your time and consideration.

Produce Business

Initial Query: July 2011
Accepted: August 2011
Published: October 2011
Paid: May 2012 (for both articles)
Fee: $384 (Pecan article); $344 (Floral QR Codes article)
Word Count: 1,500 words each
Idea:

A magazine representative, not the editor I had pitched, called me after reading my pitch below. She had an assignment about new floral marketing efforts for an upcoming issue in the magazine. (This is a trade publication for executives who make buying decisions for supermarkets.) A section of the magazine is dedicated to the floral business. As you'll see below, my pitch was unrelated to the floral market! The idea for my original pitch below came when talking to a source for a different article (see ***Vegetable Growers News***), and the source mentioned how he was innovating technology into his food marketing efforts. The pitch below never found a home, but it garnered two unrelated bylines in this magazine.

Before the magazine's representative called me, the editor emailed me back on the same day I made my pitch. He explained they rely heavily on freelancers, and he had an "exposé" with a 3-week deadline he needed a writer for. I accepted, but a week went by without hearing anything. I followed up by email and phone since it had been expressed that time was of the essence. Editorial had shifted and a different article was needed—this one on merchandising efforts for pecans in grocery stores.

Between the floral marketing piece the magazine's marketing department assigned me and the pecan merchandising piece assigned from the editor, I had two bylines with the magazine.

Sources:

The magazine provided a few contacts, and I supplemented them with sources I acquired through Help A Reporter Out.

Query:

The farm-to-fork mentality is less a trend and more a lifestyle. Consumers are conscious of traceability and food producers are responding in tech-savvy ways. Mark Thompson, a chicken farmer and creator of Eggzy.net, which is a site that connects locals with their area's flock keepers, is promoting the use of QR codes on egg cartons. QR codes, the New Age bar code, takes smartphone users to the history of the farmer, information about chickens' diets, and more products offered by the farmer. HarvestMark, a fresh food traceability platform, is a growing service distributors can use to register produce history and farm information, while allowing consumers to interact.

"The Dish on Your Dish" will be approximately 1,200 words and outline how producers are using QR codes and other trendy tech means to promote the origin of their products. The piece will also include responses restaurants receive from offering verifiable, locally-sourced dishes, feedback from food producers about how traceability features have affected sales and why consumers are willing to pay up to 50% more for local, traceable products.

Interested in this piece as a feature for *Produce Business*? I am available to discuss your ideas and thoughts. I am a full-time freelance writer based out of Raleigh, North Carolina, with features appearing or forthcoming in *GRIT, GO* (AirTran Airways' magazine) and *Triangle Gardener*. You may learn more about my work and view clips at www.taralynnegroth.com.

Thank you in advance for your time; I look forward to hearing from you.

Southern Neighbor

Initial Query: May 2009
Accepted: May 2009
Published: August 2009
Paid: August 2009
Fee: $125
Word Count: 1,200
Idea:

This was my very first successful query letter and you can see several of my novice moves in the correspondence. As mentioned early on in this book, when I first started to try and write for magazines for pay, I wrote a few articles first and then pitched. I reference one of those articles in a note below.

I saw a post on Craigslist about a publication seeking feature writers. I was not sure which publication it was, so I sent a note first to learn more. This was a smart move because then I could send a relevant pitch. In my follow-up note I included two pitches that were not very well fleshed out. I was struggling to come up with interesting articles and relied on a smart move: what I know. I tried to tie in my experiences and interests that would align with the publication's audience.

Neither of my pitches were accepted, but the editor's rejection email included an invitation to write a piece on summer festivals in the area. I received the invitation on my birthday, a great gift for my first paid article!

Sources:

I contacted entertainment venues and festival organizers associated with the festivals featured in the article.

Query:

I am writing in regards to your search for a Feature/Profile Writer that I viewed on Craigslist. I am interested in learning more about your publication. What is your readership and what are their interests? Where do you distribute? What is your message? I am a freelance writer based in Raleigh with experience in newspaper looking to branch out to magazines. I would like to formally apply for this opportunity after learning more about your publication and how my experience fits with your industry.

Thank you in advance for your time and I look forward to hearing from you.

After receiving an anonymous response with the information I requested, I followed up:

Thank you for contacting me. Attached are a few writing samples: one interview and an editorial, as well as an article I am currently pitching about locally-owned Italian restaurants in downtown Raleigh.

For your August issue I have two feature ideas for consideration. I will be volunteering at the Hog Day Festival in Hillsborough on June 20 and would like to write a piece about this event. This piece would be approximately 800-900 words featuring quotes from attendees, vendors and festival organizers with a possible side bar regarding this festival's first-ever green efforts. The second idea I have is a piece outlining the planning, efforts and tips for summer travel with your dog, cat or pet bird. I would like to quote a local veterinarian and/or doggie day care in the piece. This article will be approximately 1000 words with possible side bars noting local pet boarding facilities and a check list of items to bring along on vacation.

As per your request, my address and phone number are below. Who may be my point of contact with your publication? Let me know if you have any questions about these story ideas; I look forward to hearing from you soon. Thank you in advance for your time.

Southern Neighbor

Initial Query: July 2009
Accepted: July 2009
Published: September 2009
Paid: August 2009
Fee: $125
Word Count: 1,200
Idea:

As it was my second full year in the area, I remembered that September was full of festivals. I keep them marked on my calendar far in advance. While scrolling through the year, I noticed one weekend might make a good topic for a local publication. Since I had just finished an article with *Southern Neighbor*, I pitched the idea to them.

Sources:

I contacted festival organizers and local arts councils.

Query:

Unfortunately, this was at the time I switched email accounts and computers. I no longer have access to the letter.

Southern Neighbor

Initial Query: March 2010, approximately (I switched email accounts around this time and cannot verify the date.)
Accepted: April 2010, approximately
Published: July 2010
Paid: June 2010
Fee: $125
Word Count: 1,201
Idea:

After participating with one of the local planetarium's night paddles, I was hooked on the experience of kayaking at night. This spawned another article (see ***Blue Ridge Outdoors***), and for this one, the focus was on the stargazing angle during a guided paddle.

Sources:

I used the local planetarium program coordinator who I met on a paddle.

Query:

I hope this finds you well and you enjoyed the wonderful weather this past weekend! I was exploring Hillsborough and its "Living History Day." I also worked on a few ideas for articles and wanted to share one with you.

There's nothing quite like floating in a kayak at night with stars peppering the night sky, the moon reflected on the water's surface, and an astronomy expert pointing out "The Seven Sisters" and "Orion's Belt." It may even be the evening of a meteor shower. This is a summer night on Jordan Lake organized by the Morehead Planetarium in Chapel Hill.

"Starry, Starry Summer Nights" will be approximately 1,200 words. It will detail the "Paddling Under the Stars" program through Morehead Planetarium, offer seasonal stargazing guidance in Carolina skies as well as upcoming meteor showers, and present greater-Chapel Hill area residents a new way to spend a summer night. It will include advice from the planetarium's staff and kayak outfitters.

Interested in this piece for the July or August issue of *Southern Neighbor*? I am available to discuss your ideas and thoughts. Let me know if you have any questions about this story idea; I look forward to hearing from you soon. Thank you in advance for your time.

WOW! Women on Writing

Initial Query: February/March 2010, approximately (I switched email accounts around this time and cannot verify the exact date.)
Accepted: March 2010
Published: May 2010
Paid: May 2010
Fee: $75
Word Count: 1,592
Idea:

I started joining writing groups about a year after I moved to North Carolina. I learned about Meetup.com in the 2008–2009 timeframe and joined every writing group in my area. Almost every night of the week, I was at a different event for writers: a critique group, open mic, reading, panel, etc.

A writer chatted with me after a panel I attended at a local bookstore in Raleigh. I briefly explained about my background and interests, which were still partly in the screenwriting zone. This person immediately recommended I learn about or reach out to a screenwriter/author in the area who also works in Los Angeles.

Around this time, I received a call for submissions from *WOW*. They planned a special "Book to Film" themed issue. From what I knew about the screenwriter/author, I reflexively thought to pitch an interview with her. Also, when I looked up the writer, she had a book coming out that aligned with the theme of the *WOW* edition.

In a completely rookie move, I pitched an interview with the author to *WOW* before I even cleared the possibility with the author. Fortunately, all worked out well. *WOW* accepted my pitch, and then I promptly inquired with the author to learn if she was open to an interview—and yes, she was!

Sources:

I did an internet search for the author after I learned about her from another local writer.

Query:

Living in Los Angeles and adapting novels into screenplays for studios such as Sony and Miramax, drawing from a theatrical past of singing and acting, penning a handful of novels and numerous short stories are all notches on the belt of a Raleigh, North Carolina resident: Alexandra Sokoloff.

Sokoloff is also the author of the new e-workbook, *Screenwriting Tricks for Authors*, as well as a former member of the Board of Directors for the Writers Guild of America.

"A Writer of All Trades: An Interview with Alexandra Sokoloff" will be approximately 1,500 words. It will explore Sokoloff's background with novels and screenplays, which adaptation works best (novel to film, film to novel) and what elements screenwriting allows writers to explore that fiction limits.

Interested in this piece for the May "Book to Film" special or as a feature interview for an upcoming issue of *WOW! Women on Writing*? I am available to discuss your ideas and thoughts. I am a freelance writer residing in Cary, North Carolina, with a bachelor's degree in cinema and cultural studies. I have been published in places such as *Chesapeake Family, Southern Neighbor* and the *Providence Journal*. I also organize the Triangle Writers Group, which will be focusing on screenwriting critiques this summer. You are welcome to view clips at www.taralynnegroth.com. Also, please be advised this is an exclusive submission.

Let me know if you have any questions about this story idea; I look forward to hearing from you soon. Thank you in advance for your time.

WOW! Women on Writing

Initial Query: May 2010
Accepted: May 2010
Published: November 2010
Paid: November 2010
Fee: $150
Word Count: 1,600
Idea:

I learned about "writer insurance" while doing some research prior to publishing my guidebook to the Bonnaroo Music Festival. Media liability insurance policies help protect writers in the event they are the target of a lawsuit that occurs as a result of their writing. Many writers I spoke with had not heard about these insurance policies, and I thought it would be a good topic to cover for *WOW*.

Sources:

I was a member of The Author's Guild at the time, so I connected with their General Counsel. (FYI: When you're looking for writing organizations to join, check their member benefits for legal counsel/guidance and other perks.) The National Federation of Press Women also had a helpful contact, and I contacted representatives with the insurance companies to acquire information straight from providers.

Query:

Before one gets in their car they purchase auto insurance, when one buys a home they acquire homeowner's insurance. Journalists are notoriously concerned about health coverage polices, so why are so many writers writing without media ("writing") insurance? Because most are not aware of its existence, affordability and benefits.

"Get Covered: Media Insurance for Writers" will be approximately 1,500 words. It will outline the various benefits of media liability insurance (such as identity protection of confidential sources, coverage of copyright infringement and more), the requirements of policy holders (such as career length, income, etc.) and the costs involved (most are less than $500 annually).

Interested in this piece for your "Freelance Union 3" issue? Let me know if you have any questions about this story idea; I look forward to hearing from you soon.

Query Cemetery

Sometimes queries are accepted, but the articles are never published. Here's a little graveyard of successful query letters that died before publication.

Draft

Initial Query: August 2011
Accepted: October 2011
Killed: November 2011
Paid: February 2012
Fee: $45
Word Count: 370
Idea:

Through one of the trend-spotting services I subscribe to, I learned about a few different restaurants implementing a priceless (or price-free) dining experience. In some instances, it was to provide food for low-income individuals and families; in other situations, the model was used in hopes that patrons would pay more than what the restaurant would have charged. This notion was novel at the time, but later became a trendy marketing ploy at upscale restaurants in New York City and elsewhere.

Ultimately, the editor felt the piece leaned too heavily toward the need-based dining aspect, which didn't meld well with the mid-to-upper-income readership of the magazine. They decided not to publish it, so I inquired about a kill fee.

Sources:

I connected with the restaurants implementing the priceless menus and also found a restaurant marketing expert via Help a Reporter Out or Reporter Connection. (I'm unable to verify which network was responsible for the connection.)

Query:

What if your dinner bill was exactly what you felt it was worth? They are what you want them to be when you order from pay-what-you-can menus. Restaurants are dipping their forks into this new trend, which allows diners to contribute what they feel their meals are worth—or what their wallets allow them to pay.

Consumers are enjoying the financial freedom and eating up the meals, while restauranteurs are loving the response and dishing out more food with no prices. Restaurant owners are finding patrons pay more for meals than what the prices would have been. This is happening in northern California at Cafe Gratitude, as well as non-profit Panera locations that feature no cash registers and no prices on their menus. Some locations allow patrons to volunteer an hour of time for a meal.

"Priceless Dining" will be approximately 350 words. It will explore restaurants that are erasing prices from their menus and creating alternate options for diners to compensate for their meals. Quotes from restaurant owners and patrons will be included. The piece will also feature insight from psychologists and neuro-marketing experts about consumer response to pricing strategies.

Interested in this piece for your "On Tap Life" section in *Draft*? I am available to discuss your ideas and thoughts. I am a full-time freelance writer based out of Raleigh, North Carolina who has work featured or forthcoming in *Produce Business*, AirTran Airways' *GO Magazine* and *GRIT*. You are welcome to view clips atwww.taralynnegroth.com.

I look forward to hearing from you soon. Thank you in advance for your time.

GRIT

Initial Query: September 2015
Accepted: October 2015
Killed: November 2015

Paid: n/a
Fee: None. No contract was provided and work did not start.
Word Count: 0
Idea:

I signed up to attend a regional farm tour in my area. Agriculture is the biggest industry in Chatham County (where I live) and a big part of the surrounding area. I requested information about some farms and any notable people/advancements from the organization that runs the farm tour. Although circumstances at the last minute prevented me from attending the tour, the organization sent me a list of interesting details about the farms.

One item in particular caught my eye about a farm that recently relocated. The logistics involved with relocating a farm intrigued me and I thought would make a great article. Since I already had a connection with *GRIT*, I pitched the idea to them.

Two things to note: One, I pitched the idea in September 2015 and didn't hear back. Then I followed up (one of the key steps writers at all stages of their career need to do) a month later. The editor responded with an acceptance less than 24 hours later. She accepted the article for the November/December 2016 issue – an entire year later. Two, in ironing out the article details via email over the following month everything appeared well, but I did not receive a contract. When I requested one. I was informed that the contracts will only be sent when the issue was about to go to print.

What if there were contract terms I wanted to amend or remove? What if the terms were non-negotiable? Was I going to conduct interviews, research farms, write the article, and wait to see almost a year later if the contract the terms were acceptable? Maybe if journalism was a hobby for me then I would have been amenable to that. Instead, I explained that as a full-time writer I don't begin work on articles without a contract.

I followed up the following year and asked if I could review the contract before starting work on the article. I didn't hear back. Then in July 2016 I received an email from the editor asking if I had a draft ready of the article. I reminded her I needed to review a contract first and she said she understood and that if my policy ever changes they would like me to write the piece. Although I'm disappointed I didn't contribute this time, they were magnanimous and pleasant through all correspondence. I hope their contributor process changes so that writers can review contracts before starting work.

Sources:

I have contact information for farms that the farm tour organization connected me with, plus a few in other states I found via a simple internet search.

Query:

Relocating for a new job or family can be stressful. Furniture or sentimental items could be damaged or lost in transit, family members might get homesick, and becoming familiar with a new area takes time. What if the individual lived and worked on their farm and needed to relocate the farm? This is what sustainable Durham, North Carolina-based Bull City Farm successfully accomplished last year. Bull City Farms moved their pasture-raised sheep, cows, poultry, and bee hives along with their family. A few hundred miles up the coast, Woodstock Farm Sanctuary in Woodstock, New York relocated this year, moving sheep, cows, rabbits, poultry, and goats to a 150-acre plot - a space six-times larger than their previous land.

What are the stresses relocating farmers face? Considerably more than someone simply moving personal property and not livestock. Not only are the people living and working on the farm transitioning to a new space, but livestock must be transported safely and cared for properly so that they adjust in the best health. Plus, farms that rely on produce sales may need to adjust crop schedules to suit the labor present, climate, and soil limitations.

"Moo-ve On: Relocating a Farm, Livestock and All" will be approximately 1,200 words. It will include sources from sites like Bull City Farm and Woodstock Farm Sanctuary, among other farms in different parts of the country who have needed to relocate at some point during their operation. Business interruption and relocation requirements will be reviewed alongside animal care and preservation.

Interested in this piece as a feature for an upcoming issue of *GRIT*? I am available to discuss your thoughts. I am a full-time freelance writer based in a rural town on the outskirts of the Raleigh, North Carolina area. My work appeared in *GRIT* a few years ago: "Camel Dairy Coming Your Way" and "Digital Harvests." My other clips include *Back Home Magazine, Vegetable Growers News*, and more samples are accessible on my market inventory www.taralynnegroth.com. I am also a member of the invitation-only network of the American Society of Journalists and Authors. I maintain a flock of backyard chickens and stay connected with agricultural trends by actively attending local cooperative extension events and pollinator workshops.

Let me know if you have any questions about this idea; I look forward to hearing from you soon. Thank you in advance for your time and consideration.

Trail Runner

Initial Query: January 2012
Accepted: January 2012
Killed: April 2012
Paid: n/a
Fee: None. I decided to keep the article and shop it around.
Word Count: 854
Idea:
My mother experienced severe foot pain and was diagnosed with plantar fasciitis. It was an unexpected, painful condition that was not responding to treatments. Few proven treatments seemed to exist, but new remedies were surfacing at the time. I had been reading about them and figured I could put my research to use in an article.

Sources:

I was dating a family medicine resident at University of North Carolina-Chapel Hill at the time, and he connected me with a sports medicine professional with experience treating the condition. Help a Reporter Out helped me connect with physical therapists, authors, trail runners, and professional athletes—including Michael Sandler, the author of *Barefoot Running*.

Query:

You've been running for years. Indoors. Outdoors. You use the right shoes. Never had an injury. Most people worry about their knees, but you have no problems. You've done everything right until a constant pain in your foot develops that even keeps you awake at night. Orthotics don't work. Plantar fasciitis is a condition where the tissue on the bottom of the foot becomes inflamed. The condition sets in after long, continuous microscopic tears of the hard tissue.

In most cases, runners suffer for several months. However, a growing number of cases are becoming chronic and very few effective treatments exist. According to the *Journal of Bone and Joint Surgery*, plantar fasciitis affects two million people each year. What if a woman develops it before a family vacation? Or a runner is diagnosed with it before a triathlon? There is a new surgery currently in clinical trials using platelet replacement therapy that has proven successful for those who suffer chronic cases of plantar fasciitis.

"New Foot Pain Rx" will be approximately 800 words. The piece will explain how plantar fasciitis develops and the types of exercises that enable it. Prevention methods and traditional remedies will be included. In the past, surgeries were avoided because of the high risk for further injury and nerve damage. The article will explain how the latest surgery methods are able to skirt these issues.

Interested in this piece for the "Trail Rx" section of *Trail Runner*? I am available to discuss your ideas and thoughts. I'm a freelance writer based out of Raleigh, North Carolina, with work featured in AirTran Airways' *GO Magazine*, *Blue Ridge Outdoors* and *Chesapeake Family*. You are welcome to view clips at www.taralynnegroth.com.

I look forward to hearing your thoughts when time allows.

This Land Press

Initial Query: May 2011
Accepted: June 2011
Killed: October 2011
Paid: n/a
Fee: None. Editor offered a nominal kill fee, but I declined.
Word Count: 1,037
Idea:

I explain my background on getting introduced to camel milk dairy concepts in another article (see ***GRIT***). When the editor responded to my pitch, he asked for the focus to be on one of the farms instead of multiple farms. The article was sent in July 2011 with a $200 invoice. Editor enthusiastically sent back notes, I sent back revisions and conducted further interviews. This happened again and I obliged. Then in October, the editor decided the piece focuses too much on the one farm.

Sources:

I contacted the farmers I knew from writing previous articles. I consulted the U.S. National Library of Medicine and research publications to cite therapeutic studies.

Query:

Today there are so many choices when it comes to dairy alternatives: soy, rice, almond… but none offering more health benefits than camel milk. A low buzz has been forming over the past few years about camel milk and its cure-all properties, from diabetes to autism, even effects on virility. Plus, research is currently being conducted with the treatment of canine cancers. In respect to cow's milk, camel milk contains more vitamin C, iron and doesn't aggravate those with lactose intolerance. Camel milk reaps all the above benefits and has been shown to lower blood sugar, cholesterol and triglycerides.

A bill is currently on the table at the Food and Drug Administration (FDA) where special test kits are being formed and there are a dozen camel dairies awaiting the FDA's approval of commercial sales. Sue and Scott Menges of Stratford, Oklahoma are raising dairy camels and preparing for the commercial approval of camel milk.

"Title of the Future: Camel Farmers" will be approximately 800 words. It will bring readers a unique perspective on the the Menges' lifestyle of caring and preparing for camel dairy operation. How did they branch off into the camel milk market and what investments have they made? These questions will be answered and photos will be available as well.

Interested in this piece as a feature in *This Land Press*? I am available to discuss your ideas and thoughts. I am a full-time freelance writer residing in Cary, North Carolina who keeps a strong pulse on health trends. My work has appeared or is forthcoming in *GO* (AirTran Airways' inflight magazine), *GRIT* and the *Providence Journal.* You are welcome to view clips at www.taralynnegroth.com.

Let me know if you have any questions about this story idea; I look forward to hearing from you soon. Thank you in advance for your time.

Resources for Freelance Journalists

Here is an alphabetical listing of the resources mentioned throughout this book, plus others that can help new and long-time journalists during their careers:

American Society of Journalists and Authors – **www.asja.org**

Freelancers Union – **www.freelancersunion.org**

Help a Reporter Out (HARO) – **www.helpareporter.com**

National Association of Independent Writers and Editors – **www.naiwe.com**

National Writers Association – **www.nationalwriters.com**

National Writers Union – **www.nwu.org**

Volunteer Lawyers for the Arts – **www.vlany.org**

Volunteer Lawyers and Accountants for the Arts – **www.vlaa.org**

Writers Market – **www.writersmarket.com**

I also maintain a Resources for Writers page that I regularly update, which includes resources for both journalists and authors. You can access that page here **https://goo.gl/as8Lsy** or **http://www.taralynnegroth.com/resources-for-writers.html**. The page also includes a link to my monthly newsletter for writers, which features changes in publishing and search engine optimization, plus advance registration for my workshops and classes.

Printed in Great Britain
by Amazon